BAUDELAIRE'S SHADOW

 INVENTING WRITING THEORY

Jacques Lezra and Paul North, series editors

BAUDELAIRE'S SHADOW

AN ESSAY ON POETIC DETERMINATION

NATHAN BROWN

Fordham University Press *New York 2026*

Copyright © 2026 Fordham University Press

An earlier version of this book was published by MaMa — Multimedijalni institut (Zagreb)

All rights reserved. No part of this publication may be reproduced, stored in a retrieval system, or transmitted in any form or by any means—electronic, mechanical, photocopy, recording, or any other—except for brief quotations in printed reviews, without the prior permission of the publisher.

Fordham University Press has no responsibility for the persistence or accuracy of URLs for external or third-party Internet websites referred to in this publication and does not guarantee that any content on such websites is, or will remain, accurate or appropriate.

Fordham University Press also publishes its books in a variety of electronic formats. Some content that appears in print may not be available in electronic books.

Visit us online at www.fordhampress.com.

For EU safety / GPSR concerns: Mare Nostrum Group B.V, Doelen 72, 4831 GR Breda, The Netherlands, gpsr@mare-nostrum.co.uk

Library of Congress Cataloging-in-Publication Data available online at https://catalog.loc.gov.

Printed in the United States of America

28 27 26   5 4 3 2 1

First Fordham University Press edition

Literature is like the day: it has a morning, an afternoon, an evening and a night.
— Théophile Gautier, "Charles Baudelaire"

I want to nail my own gloomy shadow into the moonlit earth. Lest the shadow follow me forever.
— Sakutarō Hagiwara, *Howling at the Moon*

For Cynthia Mitchell,
honeybee held in the mind's eye.

Table of Contents

Preface 9

Shadow—A Parable 13

Knowledge of Nothing 55

To Look Without Loathing 103

The Existence of the Poem 159

Envoi 201

Index of Poems 205

Index 207

Preface

Baudelaire, reading. On the left, the angular rigor of the table, the cut of its corner, the consistent plane of its surface, the clear though mild illumination of its chestnut shade. On the right, the crimson repose of ample cushions, the superfluity of a tassel, an indistinct blur into the background: bohemia.

The reader, between. Book propped on one world, hand on the other. The fingers are narrow, feminine, delicately clutching with an arachnid quality to their hinged extension. The pinky drifts off on its own, at habitual or physiological remove, somatic synecdoche for a whole tendency of thought and feeling: refractory, separate in sociality, disinclined to solitude yet detached. The intensity of the gaze suggests a deliberate slowness, as if focused on each word—or, better, isolating and retaining particular signifiers. The pipe makes of the subject an atmosphere, diffusing what is interiorized. The greeny umber of the wall is of the same mood one sees in certain Delacroix clouds. The cravat, loose and sumptuous, semblable of the divan, its saffron tints holding together and punctuating the composition against the bluish white of shirt and collar. The widow's peak doubling the corner of the table, to which it points. The shadow of the book, unseen by the reader but descried by the viewer, as the words of the book are descried by the reader but unseen by the viewer: a parable of mediation. [Figure 1]

One day Baudelaire will begin a poem with a sharp, feathery adjective set apart by a bracing caesura:

FIGURE 1: Gustave Courbet, *Portrait of Baudelaire*, 1848-1849

Fière,

Two lines later, he will fold that adjective into another quality just as incisive yet more inwardly complex:

désinvolture

We could turn the description toward the figure in Courbet's portrait, insolent in concentration though possessed of a certain fluency, with the piercing ease of an ellipse, like that of the quill whose arc braces the subject and sketches the nimbus of his intellect, anticipating Brancusi.

I see it as a portrait of determination. But a portrait of *poetic* determination, sunk into the depths yet taut upon the surface, reading in order to write with all the tense patience that entails. Determination would be a quality of the soul: willful and resolute within the medium of one's fate, turning destiny toward an intentional point of concentrated focus while plunged in its unsoundable recesses. Not only the action of determining "and" the condition of being determined, but the conflicted unity of those in the essential impetus and contingent flourishes that one is, the flush of interiority that dawns as if from without. It would also be the quality of a book: set, yet mobile in its flickering passages, such that these can shape one another across intervals; a synthetic multiplicity of copies and editions, material and yet abstract, such that it can be modified to absorb new elements under the same title; transforming its reader while being transformed by reading—a singular power of action contained within an inert object.

We will leave the figure aside and attend to the task of reading, but there is something in the *way* that figure reads, distilled in this portrait, that we want to retain. All we want from Baudelaire is his book, and here it is all he wants as well. Courbet shows us with gentle insistence how to proceed: with rapt attention at once stringent and languid, fixated, but bringing to and drawing from our study a reflective interiority that half closes our eyes. A second look: is he about to nod off? How dreamy and focused is our subject, how poised and intent amid residual and incipient revery. We do indeed want to be like him, akin. We want to read and to write with the destined angularity of vocation, feeding upon desire, bringing what lies in the depths to the surface, determining it, being determined by its indeterminations, breathing them in, contemplating their clouds of significance, getting to the point.

Shadow—A Parable

"Ye who read are still among the living; but I who write shall have long since gone my way into the region of shadows."[1] Poe's "Shadow—A Parable" begins by opening a rift in time, into which falls death. On one side of the semicolon death has *not yet* taken place; on the other it has *already* happened. What enables this rift to install itself in language is writing, which makes it possible to address a reader from beyond the grave. Within the time of writing, this form of address is anticipated: "I who write" *was still* among the living. Within the time of reading, the writer's living anticipation of death ("shall have long since gone my way") is retroactively constructed: we enter into a time in which what has already happened (death) has not yet taken place, and wherein what will happen (death) has already occurred. Across the division of the semicolon, "are still" and "shall have long since" partake of a strange complicity, such that "Ye who read" pass into the region of shadows, though we are said to remain among the living. The living are determined as the remains of the dead. It is as if, within the stasis of these characters on the page, we had at once become the corpse of "I who write" and its living apparition. And how many who have read this parable are by now among the dead? How shadowed is the region of reading, how tenebrous its boundaries, as if every word one encounters were a whisper from the dark mouth of Hades.

"I who write" will be identified, in the second paragraph, as "me, the Greek Oinos." But within the opening sentence of the parable, the ontic status of this first person narrator is as yet

---

[1] Edgar Allan Poe, "Shadow—A Parable" in *Poetry and Tales*, ed. Patrick F. Quinn (New York: Library of America, 1984), 218-220. All subsequent quotations from "Shadow—A Parable" are drawn from these pages.

indeterminate. In fact, it is Poe who writes. It is he who inscribes "the characters here graven with a stylus of iron." Those whom he addresses, we who read, partake of the same modality of being as Edgar Allan Poe: we are mortal, beings who live and die, for whom life and death are not a fiction. But the fictional status of "I who write" is transcribed as a *difference* within the "I" as soon as it is written: Poe is doubled by his narrator, and his narrator by Poe, as soon as these characters are graven. This doubling immediately results in a dilation of the interval between writing and reading, as the first person narrator tells us that, by the time we read, he "shall have long since gone my way into the region of shadows." Poe wrote the tale in 1835; it was published ten years later, when he was still among the living. But how long is "long since?" As soon as Poe writes "Ye who read," he himself becomes the addressee of his writing, prior to publication: as soon as we write, we are doubled as those who read. Every writer dies, qua writer, with the inscription of every character, yet is revived as reader, to write again, through that very act of inscription. It is this *differential identity* of "I" and "Ye," implicit in the relation between writing and reading, that is shadowed by the doubling of "I who write" into factual author and fictional narrator. These redoublings are immediate: in fact there is no temporal lag between writing and reading; they are coeval with the movement of the "stylus," contracted into its point, just as is the creation of Poe's character through his own pen. But, from that point, a temporal gulf also begins to open between the time of writing and those times of reading, a multiplicity, that may lag long behind.

This gulf is expanded in the second sentence of the parable: "For indeed strange things shall happen, and secret things be known, and many centuries shall pass away, ere these memorials be seen of men." Whereas author and narrator were coevally inscribed as "I who write" within the time of the opening sentence, now they are implicitly divided by "centuries," and this gap between narrator and author amplifies that between composition and publication. Put simply, the parable is set in the past. If there is a factual interval of ten years between the composition and the publication of the text, there is a fictional interval of hundreds of years between the tale told by the narrator and its reception by readers who are Poe's contemporaries, even as there is a factual interval of one hundred and seventy years between Poe's death and my own reading of the parable. Poe's opening paragraph constructs a meditation not only upon the time of fiction and the time of reading, but upon the manner in which the former depends upon the latter to exist. Rifts in time are doubled, multiplied, and entangled, and "Ye who read" is rendered plural, differentiated according to disposition, by the final sentence of that paragraph: "And, when seen, there will be some to disbelieve, and some to doubt, and yet a few who will find much to ponder upon in the characters here graven with a stylus of iron." Presumably, we belong among those who find much to ponder, but in order to ponder Poe's parable with any lucidity we must also be among those who doubt and disbelieve: we have to understand it as a fiction. We must be "some," and "some," and yet "a few," and "ye," and even "I." We must pass into the region of shadows even as we read, *suspending* disbelief as we hover over the rift in time between the living and the dead.

The parable enters thereafter into diegetic time: "The year had been a year of terror, and of feelings more intense than terror for which there is no name upon the earth." Duration is now intensified by affect—and we will return to the depth of these nameless feelings—but for now we note the contraction of the "many centuries" elapsed since the fictional time of narration into "the year" prior to the events that will be narrated. It has been a plague year, during which "many prodigies and signs had taken place, and far and wide, over sea and land, the black wings of Pestilence were spread abroad." It is the unknown or unstated meaning of these prodigies and signs that expands the temporal frame of the parable once more—no sooner than it had been narrowed to a year—now coming to enfold not only indeterminate "centuries" but a determinate periodicity of cyclical time:

> To those, nevertheless, cunning in the stars, it was not unknown that the heavens wore an aspect of ill; and to me, the Greek Oinos, among others, it was evident that now had arrived the alternation of that seven hundred and ninety-fourth year when, at the entrance of Aries, the planet Jupiter is conjoined with the red ring of the terrible Saturnus. The peculiar spirit of the skies, if I mistake not greatly, made itself manifest, not only in the physical orb of the earth, but in the souls, imaginations, and meditations of mankind.

Cunning in the stars, our narrator knows that we have arrived at the turn of a 794 year cycle, at which the "aspect of ill" worn by the heavens affects not only the earth but also the souls of its inhabitants. Poe shuttles us from "far and wide, over sea and land" to the space of constellations, the interlocking orbits of planets, and the chromatic light of the rings of Saturn. The intensification of time by feeling undergoes an intensification of feeling by time and space: the expansion and contraction of temporal and spatial framing at once underscores, creates, and imitates the very pulsation of feeling itself, its unnamable modulations. In French there is a word for this aspect of ill at once heavenly, terrestrial, and spiritual: *ténèbres*. It designates a phenomenal state of darkness or shadow, of obscurity and fading light, that is also a condition of the soul, of imagination, and of meditations—a condition of doubt or uncertainty that links the spirit and the heavens through neither affirmation nor negation, but rather a kind of groping in the dark, an orientation toward occlusion. When Baudelaire translates "Shadow—A Parable," he titles it "*L'Ombre*," but we might also find *les ténèbres* lying beneath that translation, like a grave beneath a tombstone. For there are shadows of indetermination beneath the eponymous Shadow that will speak at the end of Poe's tale.

The first two paragraphs of the parable thus constitute a double frame—extra-diegetic and diegetic—within which the scene of the remainder will be set. The year had been a year of terror, the stars had arrived at an epochal alternation, ye who read are still among the living, and the narrator is long since dead: this is the scenario in which one arrives—after "Ye," and "I," and "those," and "me"—at the pronoun "we," which designates the shadowy figures who will occupy the tale's interior: "Over some flasks of the red Chian wine, within the walls of a noble hall, in a dim city named Ptolemais, we sat, at night, a company of seven." From now on, we are *inside* the parable, a chamber piece that unfolds through the folding together of setting and mood:

> Black draperies, likewise, in the gloomy room, shut out from our view the moon, the lurid stars, and the peopleless streets—but the boding and the memory of Evil, they would not be so excluded.

We, "a company of seven," are poised between boding and memory, expectation and recollection, and the element of this interval is Evil, which cannot be excluded. Evil *occupies* a time that is divided between the past and the future. It cannot be excluded because—unlike the moon, the lurid stars, and the peopleless streets—it is not an object. Paradoxically, it is "in" the room precisely because it does not occupy space, nor is it even present in time: Evil seems to be a psychic correlate of that constitutive division of time which gives it substance only as it recedes into memory and presses forward as anticipation.

As the synthesis of time's present-absence, its being neither here nor there yet nevertheless taking place, Evil is that which cannot be excluded since it cannot be determinately located, cannot be identifiably exteriorized. It enters into the world as a *permanent* rift in time, and thus as a kind of forgetting attendant upon the advent of memory, an indistinction subtending the presence of objects:

> There were things around us and about of which I can render no distinct account—things material and spiritual—heaviness in the atmosphere—a sense of suffocation—anxiety—and, above all, that terrible state of existence which the nervous experience when the senses are keenly living and awake, and meanwhile the powers of thought lie dormant.

Poe's punctuation begins to open stilted gaps in the text, indices of unspeakable emotional states registered by hiatus, incursions of parataxis graven with a stylus of iron. The "terrible state of existence" described by the narrator is apportioned to "the nervous," but "heaviness in the atmosphere—a sense of suffocation—anxiety," these are "things around us" that are not attached to any subject in particular. Indeed, these seem to be placeholders, metonyms, approximations of things for which the narrator "can give no distinct account." An absence of clarity and distinction characterizes narration itself, as well as that which is narrated. Poe begins by relating "Ye" and "I" across the interval of death, but now he constructs complicities of reader and writer through more subtle means than direct address. The distinctness of what is written (e.g. "heaviness in the atmosphere—a sense of suffocation—anxiety") is *said* to be indistinct, such that we are given to imagine something other than what is said around and about the narration, some other content, which must be unspeakable, on the margins of what is in fact a relatively precise description of phenomenal and emotional states. Apophasis not only declares the absence of a distinct account, it projects the presence of what supposedly cannot be accounted for, and this projected presence, inhabiting the world of the characters, migrates into the absence shadowing description—as if it were lodged beneath the dashes, as if it surrounded the subordinate clauses, as if it lay in wait somewhere beyond the end of the sentence. *There must be something else*: this "there must be" is the affective determination of rhetorical implication; this determination accompanies the telling of the tale as the tonality of the soul through which we partake of those "feelings for which there is no name upon the earth." Our mood is sewn into the parable like a thread along a seam with the needle of negation. The movement of that needle, back and forth across an interval, is "the boding and the memory of Evil" which, according to the rhetoric of apophasis, *would not* be excluded.

The assembly of the company of seven—the configuration of their bodies in the closed chamber—is delineated within the element of this negative evocation:

> A dead weight hung upon us. It hung upon our limbs—upon the household furniture—upon the goblets from which we drank; and all things were depressed, and borne down thereby—all things save only the flames of the seven iron lamps which illumined our revel. Uprearing themselves in tall slender lines of light, they thus remained burning all pallid and motionless; and in the mirror which their lustre formed upon the round table of ebony at which we sat, each of us there assembled beheld the pallor of his own countenance, and the unquiet glare in the downcast eyes of his companions.

The gravity of mood depressing all things—limbs, furniture, goblets—is interrupted by the flames of seven iron lamps that rise in "tall slender lines of light." The seven lamps literally double the seven men, since their lustre makes a mirror of the ebony table around which the company of seven sits. It is the pallid and motionless light of the seven lamps that allows each of the seven men to behold "the pallor of his own countenance" in an ebony mirror, as well as "the unquiet glare in the downcast eyes of his companions." The doubling of seven men by seven lamps doubles each of the men as his own reflection, thus doubling each of them for the others as well. The ebony table gathers the men *around it* and the lustre of the lamps *upon it*, thus redoubling the men *within it* through the illusory depth of reflection—a reflection not only of their faces but of the unquiet glare in their eyes, of their depth, of the mood that binds them. This unquiet mood is not only depressive but also manic: "Yet we laughed and were merry in our proper way—which was hysterical; and sang the songs of Anacreon—which are madness; and drank deeply—although the purple wine reminded us of blood." Merriment is hysteria, songs are madness, wine is blood. Each element of revel—laughter, song, and wine—is attended by a dire qualification like a black reflection.

What is not reflected in the parable's ebony mirror is the presence of an eighth: "For there was yet another tenant of our chamber in the person of young Zoilus. Dead, and at full length he lay, enshrouded;—the genius and the demon of the scene." *Shall have long since* was death's first phrase; now it is *yet another*: temporal precession and spatial supplement. The corpse of Zoilus counts as *one more*: he is not one of seven, yet he remains uncounted as an alteration of their number. Death is that of which one "can render no distinct account," amplifying the order of number within which it is not included, even though, like Evil, it "would not be so excluded." Zoilus is "the genius and the demon of the scene" because it is Death that draws the company of seven together, along with the dead weight of the chamber, which hangs on all its elements, as the spirit of their communion. Lying along the same horizontal plane as the surface of the ebony table, Zoilus redoubles its reflective effect insofar as his dead body is a synthesis of "each of us there assembled": just as the ebony mirror gathers into its surface, illuminated by the seven lamps, the pallor of each countenance and the downcast eyes of seven companions, the unreflected corpse condenses their destiny. Mirror and corpse: the phantasm of matter and the matter of phantasm, image and object of the living and the dead. Indeed, the corpse bears this dichotomy within its own eyes:

Alas! he bore no portion in our mirth, save that his countenance, distorted with the plague, and his eyes in which Death had but half extinguished the fire of the pestilence, seemed to take such interest in our merriment as the dead may haply take in the merriment of those who are to die.

Plague takes the place of life as the source of Heraclitean fire, here only half extinguished by Death and thus offering sufficient animation for the eyes of the dead to take an interest in those who will join them. Since "those who are to die," as we learned in the opening sentence, are none other than "Ye who read" (those *still* among the living), we too find ourselves surveyed by a disease that will survive us. The boding and the memory of Evil, unexcluded, takes the form of what will live on after it kills us: of that malediction which takes an interest in the oblivion of our merriment.

Oinos avoids the eyes of the departed, though he feels they are upon him. "Gazing down steadily into the depths of the ebony mirror," he sings, and his songs echo "afar off among the sable draperies of the chamber." But as his "loud and sonorous voice" gives out, and as those echoes "became weak, and undistinguishable, and faded away," the parable arrives at its concluding movement: "from among those sable draperies where the sounds of the song departed, there came forth a dark and undefined shadow." Poe's narrator will emphasize the ambiguity of the shadow's shape. It is "a shadow such as the moon, when low in heaven, might fashion from the figure of a man: but it was the shadow neither of man, nor of God, nor of any familiar thing." And again, "the shadow was vague, and formless, and indefinite." It is imperative, in other words, that the shadow not be an object of recognition, of representation, of reflection or redoubling. The shadow is the shadow *of nothing* and thus the shadow "of death"—that hollow interval whose designation is absented from the end of Poe's epigraph: "Yes! though I walk through the valley of the *Shadow*:   " In the absence of a name, the shadow can only say *what* (but not *who*) it is: "I am SHADOW." In being *nothing other* than itself, it is other than itself, since to be a shadow at all is to be a shadow *of*. To be a shadow *of* would be to have an origin, a cause, but it can only designate its origin by metonymy: "my dwelling is near to the Catacombs of Ptolemais, and hard by those dim plains of Helusion which border upon the foul Charonian canal." Not quite here or there, the shadow comes from somewhere "near," or "by," or "bordering upon" somewhere else. Metonymy of *where* accompanies the non-metonymy of *am*: the being of the nameless is the non-being of the name.

These puzzles of name, of place, of time, of number, and of mood are gathered into the final sentence of the parable:

> And then did we, the seven, start from our seats in horror, and stand trembling, and shuddering, and aghast: for the tones in the voice of the shadow were not the tones of any one being, but of a multitude of beings, and varying in their cadences from syllable to syllable, fell duskily upon our ears in the well remembered and familiar accents of many thousand departed friends.

The region of shadows into which "I who write" will have long since departed at the beginning of the parable returns through the voice of the shadow at its conclusion. But the tones of voice in which the shadow speaks are not those of "any one being"—not of the I who writes—"but of a multitude of beings." In arriving at the end of the parable he has inscribed with a stylus of iron, our narrator is addressed by the region to which he *was* destined (in the time of writing) and into which he *will have* entered (in the time of reading). Now this anticipatory and retroactive splitting of the I between life and death, writing and reading—which implicates as well the reader and the author of the tale—undergoes a further disjunctive synthesis, becoming a multitude. Poe's parable sets out from the duality of address

(Ye and I), complicates this through the doubling of a determinate multiple (the mirroring of seven men by seven lamps in one surface), supplements this system of reflection with "yet another" who is unreflected (the corpse of Zoilus), doubles this unreflected body with an incorporeal other (the shadow which is "neither of man, nor of God, nor of any familiar thing," yet which takes its place "over against the feet of the young Zoilus enshrouded"), and finally compounds this relay of specific and indefinite identities—of one, two, seven, fourteen, and *something* or *nothing* ("vague, formless, and indefinite")—into an indeterminate multiplicity of "tones in the voice," of many in the voice of one who is not anyone or anything in particular. And these tones are those of poetry, of literature, "varying in their cadences from syllable to syllable." The voice is a *composition* whose tones are those of a rhythmic manifold wherein the differential contribution of every element weighs in the balance. Poe's opening clause—"Ye who read are still among the living;"—is pentameter, its trochaic rhythm bespeaking the gravity of its intonation, with stresses falling upon *read* and *still*, like the stresses of a candle lit night. From syllable to syllable, Poe's parable conducts us into the region of shadows from which, as it concludes, the tones of a shadow's voice "fell duskily upon our ears in the well remembered and familiar accents of many thousand departed friends."

It is no easy matter to write and to speak, at once, in the language of the living and the dead. It takes more than one or two, more than seven, or fourteen, but also less than everything and everyone at once: it requires a complex mediation of determinacy by the indeterminate, and of indeterminacy by determination. "These brief compositions are," Poe instructs his readers, "in chief part, the results of matured purpose and very careful elaboration."[2] Constructing carefully, he will build a phantasm out of iron, and plague, and fear, and time, out of ebony mirror and sable draperies. The "supernatural" element

2 Poe, *Poetry and Tales*, 130.

of the tale emerges from the curtains into which the voice of the narrator recedes, from the fading of its echoes. The cadences of the tones of that voice fall upon our ears in "well remembered and familiar accents" because the tones that are in fact heard are not those of the shadow that speaks but of the words that are read, reproduced in the shadow of our own voice, such that the words written displace the content of what they report. As we read, the tones of what is written are given silent resonance by the whisper of subvocalization. But though it is the narrator's report that is read, not the voice of the shadow that is heard, his report nevertheless applies to itself: it is indeed the language of the dead, attributed by Oinos to the Shadow, by Poe to Oinos, by us to Poe....and by Poe to us, Ye who read? When we read, even though we are still among the living, we speak to ourselves in the language of the dead, such that the dead speak through us within the chamber of our silent meditations. To state the obvious, the apparent supernaturalism of Poe's parable is an allegory of reading. But that bare fact, emblazoned in the text's first phrase, does not suffice to convey the complexity and the intimacy of what that allegory communicates, of *how much* it says.

Indeed *how much*, or *how many*, is the question the parable ends by answering, as its final sentence moves from "we, the seven" to "many thousand departed friends"—or in Baudelaire's translation of Poe's tale, "de mille et mille amis disparus." But does anyone, or even seven someones, really have many thousand, or thousands and thousands of friends? Departure, disappearance, becomes the criterion of friendship: death. We are still among the living, but, since we will join them in the region from which they address us, we have already befriended the dead. Time is divided by mortality, but it also traverses the limits of finite life through anticipation and recollection. Time is the element of a friendship that does not end in death, which is thus a friendship that disturbs and terrifies, at least as much as it consoles: such is the testimony of writing and reading. The complex metaphysics of Poe's parable—its dread, its recessed hope, and its iron will—rests in the simplicity of this recognition. We will now follow it into the region of *Les Fleurs du Mal*.

* * *

Poe's tale of seven men supplemented by "yet another" takes place at night in a chamber whose black draperies shut out the view of peopleless streets. Baudelaire's tale of seven men shadowed by the dread of an eighth begins in the morning amid a swarming city:

> Fourmillante cité, cité pleine de rêves,
> Où le spectre en plein jour raccroche le passant!
>
> —
>
> Swarming city, city full of dreams,
> Where the specter in broad daylight seizes the passerby!³

"Les Sept Vieillards" is a strange double of "Shadow—A Parable," inverting its setting from closed chamber to city streets, from darkness to daylight, while retaining elements of its numerical determinations and sharing its sense of incipient doom. Wandering the periphery of Paris, Baudelaire's speaker encounters a singular old man, then watches as his double passes, and is then staggered to see his double followed by further copies:

---

3 Charles Baudelaire, *The Flowers of Evil*, trans. Nathan Brown (New York: Verso, 2024), 298-303. Cited hereafter as FE. This bilingual edition follows the French text of Charles Baudelaire, *Oeuvres Complètes* I, ed. Claude Pichois (Paris: Gallimard, 1975). Throughout, page numbers of complete poems in French and English are cited upon first reference, covering successive quotations from the same poem within the same chapter. When I refer to the French titles of poems or the volume, I capitalize in accordance with English-language conventions, e.g. *Les Fleurs du Mal*, "Harmonie du Soir."

À quel complot infâme étais-je donc en butte,
Ou quel méchant hasard ainsi m'humiliait?
Car je comptai sept fois, de minute en minute,
Ce sinistre vieillard qui se multipliait!

—

Of what infamous conspiracy was I the dupe,
Or what spiteful fortune would humiliate me thus?
For I counted seven times, minute by minute,
This sinister old man who multiplied himself!

It is the "eternal air" of "these seven hideous monsters" that, we are told, should elicit a "fraternal shiver" of disquiet from the reader, and that makes the speaker dread the consequences of encountering an eighth:

Aurais-je, sans mourir, contemplé le huitième,
Sosie inexorable, ironique et fatal,
Dégoûtant Phénix, fils et père lui-même?
— Mais je tournai le dos au cortège infernal.

—

Could I, without dying, have contemplated the eighth,
Inexorable copy, ironic and fatal,
Disgusting Phoenix, self-same father and son?
—But I turned my back on the infernal procession.

As the corpse of Zoilus mediates between the seven men and their encounter with the multitudes of the shadow's voice, the unbearable prospect of an eighth old man mediates between the series of seven and its potentially infinite expansion. Poe leaves the corpse uncounted, merely referring to it as "yet another," but Baudelaire's translation of the tale assigns it a number: "Car il y avait dans la chambre un huitième personnage, —le jeune Zoïlus."⁴ Different as they are, what Poe's parable and Baudelaire's poem have in common is that each involves a passage from a group of seven to an eighth (linked with a corpse or the possibility of death), and in each case this supplement to a numerically determinate plurality mediates a disturbing passage from the individuality of *one being* to the indeterminacy of a *multitude of beings*.

Here is Baudelaire's translation of the key passage in Poe:

> Et alors, touts les sept, nous nous dressâmes d'horreur sur nos sieges, et nous nous tenion tremblants, frissonants, effarés; car le timbre de la voix de l'ombre n'était pas le timbre d'un seul individu, mais d'une multitude d'êtres....⁵

"Shadow—A Parable" and "The Seven Old Men" share a fraternal shiver at the advent of this multitude—at the "thousands and thousands" speaking through the voice of a shadow and at the "infernal procession" of an "inexorable copy" whose reproduction can only be halted by turning away. They share this fraternal shiver, as well, with the procession of ghosts in Macbeth to which commentators have pointed as a source for Baudelaire's poem:

> Thou art too like the spirit of Banquo. Down!
> Thy crown does sear mine eyeballs. And thy hair,
> Thou other gold-bound brow, is like the first.
> And a third is like the former. Filthy hags,
> Why do you show me this? A fourth? Start, eyes!
> What, will the line stretch out to th' crack of doom?
> Another yet? A seventh? I'll see no more.

---

4 Charles Baudelaire, trans., "Ombre" in *Edgar Allan Poe: Oeuvres en Prose*, ed. Y.-G. Le Dantec (Paris: Gallimard, 1951), 478.

5 Baudelaire, trans., "Ombre," 479.

And yet the eighth appears, who bears a glass
Which shows me many more...[6]

Here again we find the movement from seven to eight giving way onto an indeterminate multiplicity of "many more," and we find this movement accompanied by horror. "Thou art too like"—this can be true of texts as well as ghosts.

What is the meaning of this fraternal shiver? What nameless feelings does it express? Why are these expressed through this peculiar relation between individuality ("I"), a determinate multiple ("seven"), a disturbing supplement ("yet another"; "the eighth"), and an indeterminate multiplicity ("a multitude of beings")? There is certainly no reason *not* to think that Baudelaire's poem is influenced by a text he translated and an author he claimed as his *semblable*. As a reader of Poe, as the writer of Poe into French, Baudelaire positions himself and his double within the complicity of reading and writing, their retroactive and projective codetermination: "Do you know why I translated Poe so patiently? Because he resembled me. The first time I opened one of his books, I saw, with dread and delight, not only subjects that I had dreamt of, but certain SENTENCES conceived by me and written by him twenty years before."[7] Poe's writing is the mime of Baudelaire's reading of Poe; Baudelaire's reading of Poe is the retrospective recognition of his own writing. The metaphysical puzzles of the texts they compose, traversing the distinction between the living and the dead through allegories of reading, are also those of their likeness. But we will be less concerned with the question of influence than with the metaphysical problem lodged in a structure, and with the affective correlate of that problem. The question is not whether one of

---

6 William Shakespeare, *Macbeth*, IV.1.134-242, ed. Stephen Orgel (New York: Penguin, 2000), 67.

7 Charles Baudelaire to Théophile Thoré, June 1864, in *Correspondance* II, ed. Claude Pichois and Jean Ziegler (Paris: Gallimard, 1973), 386. My translation.

these texts is directly influenced by another (a question dependent on a linear temporality Baudelaire's own formulation inverts and displaces), but rather how we should understand the *sense* of numerical determination they have in common.

Why seven? One wants to say it doesn't really matter, but it would seem difficult not to be troubled by this question while reading Poe's tale, in which the number is repeated with a curious insistence. Does "the alternation of that seven hundred and ninety-fourth year" divide into seven? No. Does it divide into eight? No. And what if it did? There will be some who disbelieve, and some who doubt, and some who ponder the determinate significance of such details.

But they do pose the problem of *determinate significance*. We begin reading the parable and we encounter the number seven hundred and ninety-four in the second paragraph. It is as though the number seven then drops out into the paragraph below: "we sat, at night, a company of seven." It repeats in the description of "the seven iron lamps that illumined our revel" and is reiterated again, twice, toward the end of the tale: "we, the seven there assembled"; "and then did we, the seven, start from our seats in horror." We then come to understand from the tale's concluding sentence that we have been reading a parable about the distinction between the one and the many, one being and a multitude of beings. Where does the determinate plurality of seven fit into that distinction? Where does its supplement, corpse or shadow, fall?

The assignment of a determinate *number* to the first person plural—"we"—poses an unavoidable interpretive problem, but one it would likely be foolish to try to solve. Thus it constructs a double bind, or sets a trap. The commentator could refer to numerology, to biblical significance, to occult practices, to the order of prime numbers, etc. None of these would be irrelevant, but nor would the information provided tell us anything *determinate* about the tale. The determinacy of the number presses home the indeterminacy of its interpretation, but that would be true of any number, and urbane, reflexive recognition of this interpretive problem offers little satisfaction. It is more to the point that seven is the *kind* of number that raises these questions; it *seems* significant. It is this kind of seeming that is used to advantage by both Poe and Baudelaire. The number is accompanied by a mood. Creating a nimbus of suggestion, it provokes occult researches through which the certainty of possibilities (it *can* mean this or that) is accompanied by the suspension of interpretive commitment (it *may not* mean this or that, or anything at all), and this *feels* a certain way. One gropes toward the assignment of a meaning in which one will not quite be able to believe; one acknowledges that the assignment of meaning would be arbitrary, and one then settles for a reflexive, dialectical comprehension of this oscillation. But the process is unsettling. It cannot but hold in store the possibility that we have missed something, that we are insufficiently informed, that even in sidestepping a trap we are the butt of a more elaborate joke, and thus it points up the paranoid nature of interpretation and indeed of reading: *this means something...*

Far from dissolving the problem of the number's determinate significance, this *is* its determinate significance: we are drawn into "the mystery and absurdity" by which Baudelaire's speaker is wounded as he retreats from the streets and locks himself into his room. Among the most influential papers in the history of psychology is G.A. Miller's analysis of the quantitative "span of absolute judgment" and the "span of immediate memory," in which he notes that these are "somewhere in the neighborhood of seven" items. The paper concludes as follows:

> And finally, what about the magical number seven? What about the seven wonders of the world, the seven seas, the seven deadly sins, the seven daughters of Atlas in the Pleiades, the seven ages of man, the seven levels of hell, the seven primary colors, the seven notes of the musical scale, and the seven days of the week? What about the seven-point

rating scale, the seven categories for absolute judgment, the seven objects in the span of attention, and the seven digits in the span of immediate memory? For the present I propose to withhold judgment. Perhaps there is something deep and profound behind all these sevens, something just calling out for us to discover it. But I suspect that it is only a pernicious, Pythagorean coincidence.[8]

Miller relegates the recurrence of this number to the status of coincidence, yet he nevertheless feels it is a *pernicious* coincidence due to its effects on his own psyche, which has been subjected to "malicious persecutions" by the number seven in the course of his research.[9] His paper opens with a confession: "My problem is that I have been persecuted by an integer."[10]

To be persecuted by an integer is to truly *encounter* it, such that the encounter begins to haunt your dreams, pursue you, to sink in its teeth. And it is not every day that one really encounters a number. Baudelaire arranges this encounter on our behalf. An encounter is that which simply *happens*, but it is the special capacity of literature to *make it happen*, to construct the encounter, to determine contingency while still rendering determination contingent. Poe constructs our encounter with SHADOW, which turns out to be an encounter with the multitude of the dead. Baudelaire constructs an encounter with the "eternal," and it matters less that seven may be "symbolic" of perfection, that eight may be "symbolic" of eternity, than that it is the potential but avoided passage between those numbers, within the poem itself, that actually gives us to think what eternity *is*.

Baudelaire's construction is formally elaborate. The poem opens with three introductory quatrains, in which the speaker's

8 G.A. Miller, "The Magical Number Seven, Plus or Minus Two Some Limits on Our Capacity for Processing Information," *Psychological Review* 63.2 (1956): 81-97. 96.
9 Miller, "Magical Number Seven," 91.
10 Miller, "Magical Number Seven," 81.

perambulations around the city are evoked through a dense network of figures: the city is full of dreams; mysteries seep through it like sap; the streets through which they seep are like the pinched arteries of a colossus. Houses whose appearance is elongated by haze simulate two quays of a swollen river; the filthy yellow fog is scenery akin to an actor's soul; the protagonist steels his nerves like a hero, and as he walks he bickers with his already weary soul as though it were a long-suffering spouse or an old friend. The speaker is doubled; he confers with himself. The city is multiplied; it swarms with images of its compound nature. Yet both speaker and city are quotidian: the periphery rumbles with the passage of loaded carts, the poet's soul is heavy and grumbling. It is in this atmosphere of quotidian burden that we encounter an old man.

If the filthy yellow fog flooding the streets is "scenery akin to an actor's soul" then our encounter is a *coup de théâtre*, anticipated (or instantiated?) by the phrase "Tout à coup," which inaugurates the fourth quatrain. From this "All of a sudden" we will count seven quatrains during which the old man and his multiples are described, before the speaker turns his back on the procession in the first of three quatrains concluding the poem. Beginning, middle, end (3 + 7 + 3 = 13): a tale of bad luck, told. The transitions between these sections are telling. Fourth strophe: "Tout à coup, un vieillard...." Eleventh strophe: "Aurais-je, sans mourir, contemplè le huitème...." We are introduced to an old man without warning, as if he comes out of nowhere. He is described and replicated over seven quatrains, concluding with an insistence on the "eternal air" of these "seven hideous monsters." Then the old man vanishes from the poem in the next quatrain, the eighth after his introduction, as the contemplation of an eighth copy is attended by the prospect of death. The poem thus doubles the content of its numerical figures with its form, such that the number seven is hidden within its structure, though hidden in broad daylight.

We begin to read: we are reading the *first* strophe. The poem begins, and then we traverse one of its parts; we count it as one. One is underway, and then it *counts* as one, as we pass onto two. We read the second strophe, itself one unit, and now we have traversed two elements of a structure. We read the third, after which the poem's focus on the city and the speaker are interrupted by a break, *tout à coup*. Now we might retroactively designate a set of units, a set of three, which constitutes an introduction, while we start anew in strophe four. In our paranoid fashion, we may add the numerals assigned these elements: we encounter the old man as we pass from three to four, and 3 + 4 = 7. We now pass through seven quatrains describing the old man's appearance and his replication, before the speaker turns his back and the poem concludes with three quatrains bookending those seven strophes at its center.

This is a description of structure: the poem opens with an introductory section of three strophes and concludes with three strophes enclosing a central section of seven, in which an old man and his multiples are encountered and described. We could add a description of form: "The Seven Old Men" is a narrative poem of thirteen quatrains composed of alexandrines set in alternate rhyme. But the implicit count in which form and structure are implicated, as they unfold in the time of writing and reading, will not allow form and structure to be detached from their genesis. The poem embodies this genesis; as an inscription, it holds it in place. But the *sense* of that inscription undergoes a process of genesis whenever it is read, whenever we return to it, interrupting or engaging it here or there, holding it up to our attention and turning it over and around like a gem with a certain number of facets. We can vary the phenomena of its refractions, empirically or eidetically, yet they are also possessed of a structural objectivity. "*Tout* est nombre," Baudelaire writes in *Fusées*; "Le nombre est dans *tout*. Le nombre est dans l'individu. L'ivresse est un nombre." ("*Everything* is number. Number is in the individual. Drunkenness is a number.")[11] Drunkenness is a number because it is a question of *how much*, of *how many* drinks one has had. 1, 2, 3, 4...how many suffice for the advent of the daylight specter, whose phantasm renders one "Exaspéré comme un ivrogne qui voit double"? Number is in the individual because it is a matter of *determination*, of those mediations of quantity and quality that individuate the particular. *What* and *how* are also always a question of *how much* and *how many*.

Baudelaire's poem unfolds through such mediations of quantity and quality, becomes what it is through the elaborately structured procession of its narrative. The first mediation of quantity and quality that we encounter is *saturation*. The city is "swarming," it is "full," and mysteries seep "everywhere." Immediately, quantity is pushed to the limit, and the quality of this immersion in plenitude is constriction: the city is huge, a colossus, but its arteries are pinched. This saturation of the opening quatrain is relayed and intensified not only by the density of the images, but also by the circuitous passageways of grammar, as Baudelaire's sentences wind across lines and through subordinate clauses in the following two strophes:

> Un matin, cependant que dans la triste rue
> Les maisons, dont la brume allongeait la hauteur,
> Simulaient les deux quais d'une rivière accrue,
> Et que, décor semblable à l'âme de l'acteur,
>
> Un brouillard sale et jaune inondait tout l'espace,
> Je suivais, roidissant mes nerfs comme un héros
> Et discutant avec mon âme déjà lasse,
> Le faubourg secoué par les lourds tombereaux.
>
> ——
>
> One morning, while in the dismal street

[11] Charles Baudelaire, *Fusées* in *Oeuvres Complètes* I, ed. Claude Pichois (Paris: Gallimard, 1975), 649. My translation.

> The houses, stretched high by the haze,
> Were simulating two quays of a swollen river,
> And while, scenery akin to an actor's soul,
>
> A filthy yellow fog flooded the space,
> I traced, steeling my nerves like a hero
> And bickering with my long-suffering soul,
> The neighborhood shaken by carts loaded down.

Saturation is combined with suspension: the "swollen river" concentrates this relation as image, while grammar activates it at the level of narrative. It is *the subject*, both the reader and the speaker, whose narrative progress is suspended by hypotaxis: "One morning, ... / ..., ..., / ... ..., / ..., ..., / ... ..., / I traced, ... / ...., / The neighborhood...." Through twists and turns of grammar suspending narrative, we shuttle swiftly between quantitative terms that collect and disperse elements of that narrative into unities, pluralities, and indeterminate volumes: *un* matin, *la* triste rue, *les* maisons, *la* brume, *les* deux quais, *une* rivière, *une* brouillard, *tout* l'espace. Meanwhile, doubles already proliferate: the stretched houses *simulate* the quays; the decor is the *semblable* of the soul. All this takes place in one sentence, stretched across two strophes that lock into place with a full stop following "les lourds tombereaux." The street is *dismal*, houses are *elongated*, the river is *swollen*, the fog is *filthy*, the nerves are *steeled*, the carts are *loaded*. These are strophes weighty with mediations of quantity and quality, saturated by their codeterminations of experience.

Baudelaire's elaborate grammatical suspensions are integral to his style, to the capacity of his poems to render the complexity of phenomenal experience and its mediation by memory. One of his simplest and most tender poems records the intimate qualifications of a single sentence as it gathers and refracts the time of what is not forgotten:

> Je n'ai pas oublié, voisine de la ville,
> Notre blanche maison, petite mais tranquille;
> Sa Pomone de plâtre et sa vieille Vénus
> Dans un bosquet chétif chachant leurs membres nus,
> Et le soleil, le soir, ruisselant et superbe,
> Qui, derrière la vitre où se brisait sa gerbe,
> Semblait, grand œil ouvert dans le ciel curieux,
> Contempler nos dîners longs et silencieux,
> Répandant largement ses beaux reflets de cierge
> Sur la nappe frugale et les rideaux de serge.
>
> —
>
> I have not forgotten, next to the city,
> Our white house, little but tranquil;
> Its plaster Pomona and its elderly Venus
> In a meager copse hiding their naked members,
> And the sun, in the evening, streaming down and superb,
> Which, behind the pane where its sheaf would shatter,
> Seemed, great open eye in the curious sky,
> To contemplate our long and silent dinners,
> Spreading widely its beautiful candle reflections
> Upon the frugal cloth and the serge curtains.[12]

The lyric "I" begins as the subject of the poem, the tranquil house its recollected object. But both cede pride of place to the sun, which mediates their relation as its refractions stream through the window to illuminate the interior, becoming in its own right a lyric subject through its contemplation of "our long and silent dinners." The modesty of the plaster Pomona and elderly Venus, of their meager copse, is matched by the frugal tablecloth, such that the splendor of the poem and the life it recalls does not reside in the luxury of commodities, nor of "nature," but of the strange communion of that which is "little but tranquil" with the superb light of the sun, which costs nothing, is simply given.

12 FE, 334–335.

The elderly remnants of antiquity reside within a lost garden which is not a distant Eden but rather "voisine de la ville," on the periphery of the modern. The sentence wends its way through the unforgotten, accumulating particulars which are rendered both quotidian and superb by the poem's mellow illuminations, wherein sun and candle become one: their reflections are beautiful. Baudelaire writes to his mother in 1858: "Vous n'avez donc pas remarqué qu'il y avait dans Les Fleurs du mal deux pièces vous concernant, ou du moins allusionnels à des détails intimes de notre ancienne vie, de cette époque de veuvage qui m'a laissé de singuliers et tristes souvenirs...?" ("Have you not noticed that in Les Fleurs du Mal there are two pieces concerning you, or at least alluding to intimate details of our old life, of that period of widowhood which has left me with singular and sad memories...?").[13] I have not forgotten.... Have you not noticed? Have you not noticed that I have not forgotten? The sentence is the medium of memory, as the suspensions of its grammar gather "intimate memories," sad and singular, into the complex and accumulated time of a recollection that wants to be read, to be remembered in common.

 We are proximate to this poem at the outset of "The Seven Old Men," as the speaker traces the periphery, "voisine de la ville." But long and silent dinners have been displaced by rumbling carts, the meager copse by pinched arteries, and beautiful wide reflections with a filthy yellow fog. The tender recollections of "I have not forgotten..." have been filtered through the bitter memories of "The Enemy":

> Ma jeunesse ne fut qu'un ténébreux orage,
> Traversé çà et là par de brillants soleils;
> Le tonnerre et la pluie ont fait un tel ravage,
> Qu'il reste en mon jardin bien peu de fruits vermeils.

---

[13] Charles Baudelaire, *Correspondance* II, ed. Claude Pichois and Jean Ziegler (Paris: Gallimard, 1973), 445.

> My youth was nothing but a tenebrous storm,
> Crossed here and there by shafts of sun;
> Thunder and rain have wreaked such ruin,
> That few blushing fruits remain in my grove.[14]

This is the mood of memory disenchanted. But if the lyric subject who passes through the "city full of dreams" at the outset of "The Seven Old Men" has been cast outside the intimacy of "les choses intimes de famille," the pinched arteries he traces are still rendered in sentences that beautifully suspend the details they accumulate. We can imagine that the long-suffering soul we encounter is still that which had felt itself observed, some twenty years earlier, by the great open eye in the curious sky. It is precisely *this* synthesis of the subject, the gathering of the past into the present as it stems into the future, that will be interrupted by the advent of the old man.

Through the saturated passages and narrative suspensions of its introductory strophes, Baudelaire's sentences draw us into the poem. They draw us in because in order to read the poem we have to inhabit it, not merely reflect upon or interpret it. We encounter the *existence* of the poem not only as a finished artifact but also as a relational world: a spatially extended, temporally rhythmic, physically inscribed, tonally singular, affectively generative, and semiotically rich experience. The experience of the poem's existence demands attention to *poiesis* as processual determination, not merely by authorial construction but by the way in which the poem *takes place* as the construction that it is, through the extension of its temporalization. Such a methodological orientation is not in conflict with "formalism;" by taking seriously the question what form *is*, of how it exists, we enter into those mediating determinations of which it is made.

---

14 FE, 76–77.

What the existence of the poem requires of us, as critics, is not that we offer an account of *our* experience of the poem but rather of *the* experience of the poem. The *discipline* of a critical relation to reading entails observing our observations as they appear and considering their relevance not simply in terms of whether they are arbitrary or essential—for they are never one or the other—but in terms of their determinations: from whence do they arise, and precisely how is their emergence constrained and mediated by the poem? Can we draw from an account of what happens in the poem an account of the way it works? Of how its determinations mediate and configure, how they construct our thinking and feeling? Saturation and suspension, through figuration and grammar, are the means by which the introductory section of this poem prepares us for an encounter by deferring its advent while immersing us in a mood. In order to be "persecuted by an integer," to be accosted by quantity, we have to undergo a saturation of qualities: shimmerings of haze, transmutations of scenery, the filth of yellow fog, the rumbling of carts which accompany disputations of the I with the soul, of "Je" and "mon âme." Fusing quantity and quality by rendering qualities *replete* with determination, and by suspending narrative development so as to render it qualitatively dense: these techniques prepare the ground for an interruption, for the ungrounding of narrative by event, *tout à coup*.

    The qualitative manifold of the world, the swarming multiplicity of phenomena so intricately described as the poem opens, is interrupted by *one* thing that appears in that world. The qualities of this being subsume the poem, backgrounding all that was foreground. The exterior scenery of the city and the interior disputations of the hero with his soul are drawn into and thereby displaced by the delineation of a single figure: his yellow rags mimic the color of the rainy sky and the anxiety of the speaker is projected into the malice gleaming in the man's eyes. Having subsumed these elements of the poem's introduction, the old man takes center stage for the next seven strophes. Is it at the stroke of noon that the old man steps into the poem, all of a sudden? The poem begins in the morning, but what time is it when something *happens*, when the encounter takes place? *How many* hours pass as the speaker bickers with his soul and carts rumble through the streets? *How much* time has gone by? Even before the old man multiplies, he emerges from these questions: *how many? how much?* Before they pertain to an inexorable copy, these questions are implicitly posed of the missing time from which the old man emerges. The pure advent of his appearance stems from a rift within time that opens amid a saturated world.

To return to our claim above, what the appearance of the old man interrupts is the temporal synthesis of the subject: the continuum of identity within which the speaker confers with his soul. "I" and "soul" are two, engaged in a tête-à-tête amid their passage through the city, but for "I" and "soul" to communicate they have to be one, synthesized as a subject who can talk to himself. The old man steps into the poem as if from the future: what the speaker *will be* is here *even now*, detached from the synthesis of past and future that held the subject together in and as the present. It is imperative, however, that we understand the figural advent of the speaker's future ("an old man") as erupting from within a gap that was already the principle of temporal continuity across difference: it happens both all at once and across the suspensions of a sentence, across a break between strophes. There must be an interval of time, across which continuity stretches, in order for there to be a *synthesis* of the subject at all. Time is a divided continuum, never present to itself: the old man is both a manifestation of this quotidian situation and a defamiliarization of its implications.

Let us look more closely at his introduction:

Tout à coup, un vieillard dont les guenilles jaunes
Imitaient la couleur de ce ciel pluvieux,
Et dont l'aspect aurait fait pleuvoir les aumônes,
Sans la méchanceté qui luisait dans les yeux,

M'apparut.

—

Suddenly, an old man whose yellow rags
Mimicked the color of the rainy sky,
And whose aspect would have drawn showers of alms,
Were it not for the malice that gleamed in his eyes,

Appeared.

In the opening quatrains, the speaker of the poem had been introduced across the interval between "Un matin" and "Je suivais." The old man shows up all at once ("Tout à coup, un vieillard"), but the verb required to complete the sentence is suspended across three lines and across a break between strophes. He appears *immediately*, but his appearance ("M'apparut") is also *mediated* by a deferral composed of predicates. These predicates are consistent with the atmosphere of the city (they imitate it), but their combination is inconsistent with integration into its social codes, and also inconsistent among themselves: his appearance *would* yield alms, *were it not* for the malicious gleam in his eyes. Incompatible with charity, the malice in the man's eyes is also incompatible with his own "aspect." He too is divided, his appearance suspended across the description of his predicates, but while the speaker is introduced as one who follows or traces ("Je suivais"), the old man simply appears as one who appears. Later it will be *he* who is followed by his double.

A disjunction thus appears within the verb "suivre." The lyric speaker talks to himself and traces the outskirts, follows the periphery of the city. "Je" confers with "mon âme," implying their separation, but the body's movement through space is the site of their synthesis: they follow as one. The multiplication of the old man into a double spatializes the temporal split which is synthesized in the subject, such that his body, his *appearance*, follows itself. The multiples that march in step with the old man are a spatialized figure of temporal succession which now duplicates and multiplies, rather than unifies, the subject, unravelling the synthesis of "I" and "soul" across their separation.

This figural dislocation of synthesis encodes a perennial question: how can I, right now, be the same person I will be in the future? How can the one I will be in the future be the same as the one I was in the past? These questions are implicit in the query subtending the riddle of the sphinx—What is man?—which is relayed by the poem:

> Il n'était pas voûté, mais cassé, son échine
> Faisant avec sa jambe un parfait angle droit,
> Si bien qu son bâton, parachevant sa mine,
> Lui donnait la tournure et le pas maladroit
>
> D'un quadrupède infirme ou d'un juif à trois pattes.
>
> —
>
> He was not bent, but broken, his spine
> Forming a perfect right angle with his leg,
> So that his cane, the finishing touch,
> Gave him the shape and the faltering step
>
> Of an infirm quadruped or a three-legged Jew.

The body of the old man is the spatialization of a temporal structure that "was not bent, but broken." As a geometrical figure, he approximates, or falters between, quadrilateral and triangle. He thus joins, with a faltering step, the infant and the old man of the Oedipal riddle, wherein the speaker would take his place as the synthesis of these, situated in the middle of life's way. But instead of *being* the synthesis of what he has been and will be, the I observes, with disquiet, a disjunction of that synthesis which intervenes from the future, within the rift that had already opened between "I" and "my soul" as morning drifted toward high noon. In truth, that rift has already opened as soon as we are thrown into the world, *tout à coup*.

Here we might consider a curious duplicity in the function of the imagination that is foregrounded by the Kantian theory of the subject. On the one hand, "imagination is the faculty of representing an object in intuition even without its presence."[15] It is the faculty which brings forth "the specter in broad daylight," which can produce images of what is not given in experience. On the other hand, imagination is the faculty of "synthesis in general"—that "blind but indispensable function of the soul without which we should have no knowledge whatsoever, but of which we are scarcely ever conscious."[16] Sensation is *given* to intuition, within the forms of space and time. The manifold of intuition is *synthesized* by the imagination, then brought under concepts of the understanding that determine objects as unities. Through the function of synthesis, imagination mediates between the given and the known, between pure sensations and objects of experience. Above all, the imagination synthesizes the *subject* of experience: "By means of pure imagination we bring the manifold of intuition on one side into connection with the necessary unity of apperception on the other."[17] It is through the imagination's function of synthesis that the "I think" of pure apperception is brought into connection with the givenness of the world, and this synthesis mediates the construction of experience as knowledge of objects. Imagination is the faculty of mediation between the intellectual and the sensible. Moreover,

15 Immanuel Kant, *Critique of Pure Reason*, trans. Marcus Weigelt (New York: Penguin, 2007), B151. Cited hereafter as CPR.
16 Kant, CPR, A78/B103.
17 Kant, CPR, A124.

this mediation is constitutively *temporal*: imagination synthesizes the time of inner sense (of subjective interiority) with the temporal determination of objects of experience.

What happens in Baudelaire's poem is that the first function of imagination mentioned above—the production of images in the absence of objects—is unhinged from the second function of imagination: the synthesis of the subject. The imagination produces an image of the subject shorn of synthesis, and this image, taken as an object of experience, *interrupts* the synthesis of the subject. Indeed, the production of representations of objects in the absence of subjective unity is something akin to psychosis: hallucinations are a derangement of imagination's function, wherein subjective synthesis cannot hold together representations that are not *given* to intuition but produced without the presence of an object. But we are not dealing here with actual hallucinations; we are dealing with the literary representation *of* a hallucination constructed with perfect rigor by a writer—such is the testimony of the verse itself—in perfect control of his faculties.

We can be more precise, calling again upon the assistance of Kant. What happens in Baudelaire's poem is that the *schema* of temporal synthesis is itself presented as the *image* of a rift in time. That of which there can be no image, since it is the ground of all images, is presented as the image of groundlessness: a displacement of temporal synthesis that takes place in time.

What Kant calls a transcendental schema is a "transcendental time determination," a *structure* of temporal determination that mediates between concepts and appearances, thus endowing the latter with unity. The schema is that which determines the unity of sensibility in accordance with certain principles. In experience, the given is always there, such that in all change there is *permanence*. Experience is *successive*, such that alternations proceed according to connections of cause and effect. It is *simultaneous*, insofar as determinations of successive states occur together, in a thoroughgoing interaction. These are synthetic principles Kant allocates to the pure understanding, and they are connected with determinations of experience, with the givenness of intuitions, through the schematizing function of imagination, which applies these temporal principles to the flux of sensation.

"The schema," Kant writes, "in itself is always only a product of the imagination; but as the synthesis of imagination does not aim at a single intuition, but only at the unity of the determination of sensibility, the schema ought to be distinguished from the image."[18] Let us unpack this dense formulation. Sensations are given in perpetual flux, yet they are unified in perception. It is the function of a temporal schema to determine their unity. This unity is not that of a *single* image; it is the synthesis of a manifold. The schema is thus that "through which and according to which images first become possible": the unity of images is made possible by a synthesis of time.[19] Whether they are representations of objects that are *given* or whether such representations are *produced* by imagination without the presence of an object, images rely for their unity upon the determination of a schema linking concepts to intuitions through transcendental time determinations (permanence, succession, simultaneity).

The schema *ought* to be distinguished from the image, but in Baudelaire's poem it is not. Temporal succession, which should be invisible, is directly produced as an image: the reproduction of the old man. Moreover, the "thoroughgoing interaction of successive states" is broken: there is no causal integration of the figure's duplication. The simultaneity of succession, which should synthesized as the unity of the subject (permanence) takes the form of disjunctive *replication*. The permanence of the subject across time is fragmented into an "inexorable copy." That is, the very principles which govern the synthesis of experience—and through which the subject of experience is itself synthesized—are not mediated by a schema, but immediately

18 Kant, CPR, A140/B179.
19 Kant, CPR, A142/B181.

produced as images. Time itself becomes image. The imagination produces an image of the rift within the subject that *ought* to be drawn together through the synthesis of the imagination, but instead the two functions of imagination collapse, producing an image of the default of synthesis. Considered within the diegesis of the poem, this is a matter of considerable mental distress. Because a default of synthesis renders the world *senseless*, the subject can only make sense of his experience by assuming he is the dupe of an infamous conspiracy, that he is the victim of spiteful fortune. He offers causal explanations of acausal phenomena. Considered in terms of the order of the poem as a literary object, its figure of the collapse of the imagination's two functions is also the figure of imagination's limit and its highest power: the representation of its own derangement.

We can now understand just why we should share a fraternal shiver at the "eternal air" of which these multiples are possessed, despite their decrepitude. "All appearances are in time, and in it alone (as permanent form of intuition) can simultaneity as well as succession be represented. Time, therefore, in which all change of appearances is to be thought, endures and does not change."[20] To represent the *form* of intuition, rather than appearances within it, is to represent that which does not change. Appearing within a gap in succession and simultaneity—*Tout à coup...M'apparut*—the old man makes manifest this strange "aspect" of time itself, as that which does not change amid the flux of appearances, since it constitutes their form. But to offer an image of the *permanence* of time while still offering an image of the permanence *of time*, one would have to make it repeat. Succession, simultaneity, and permanence can be represented *at once* only as an inexorable copy. The man appears "minute by minute," but he is always the same. "This sinister old man who multiplied himself" could only be a figure of time itself, and this is what lends him the air of eternity: his self-same replication is the figure of time as that which does not change.

20 Kant, CPR, A181/B225.

But we have to go further yet. This is not only an image of time in general but of, in particular, the time *of the subject*, which is why Kant is an apt guide. That subject who has not forgotten, who projects ahead, and who bickers with his soul in the middle of life's journey—this subject now sees his future self with malice gleaming in its eyes. *If time itself is represented, it cannot be represented only as form but must also be represented as content, as image.* Here this image takes the form of time's most intimate content, the inner sense. It is subjective interiority that is exteriorized as image, not as subjective "expression" but as the *essence* of subjective interiority. Time is at once the difference between "I" and my "soul" *and* the synthetic form that binds them together as I trace my course. Baudelaire sees, however, that this minimal difference, the constitutive division of time, lies at the core of the riddle of the sphinx. It poses the question of how three can be one, such that we might also ask how three plus one can be four, of how three plus four can be seven. How does addition constitute unity? Seven plus one... *How long* will I live, and *how many* can I endure? Will I die if seven plus one adds up to eight? How many is too much when the unity of synthesis is broken?

Mortally threatened by the question, our speaker turns his back on the "cortège infernal." And Baudelaire is explicit: the *inescapability* of time itself, here drawn out of the subjective rift upon which its synthesis relies, is hell:

Son pareil le suivant: barbe, œil, dos, bâton, loques,
Nul trait ne distinguait, du même enfer venu,
Ce jumeau centenaire, et ces spectres baroques
Marchaient du même pas vers un but inconnu.

—

His double followed him: beard, eye, back, cane, rags,
No trait distinguished them, come from the same hell,
This centenarian twin, and these baroque specters
Marched in step to an unknown end.

The virtuosic mastery of the alexandrine in these lines is itself disconcerting, as we flow through the sibilants of "Son pareil le suivant" into an abrupt caesura, matching form to content as it is followed by the limping succession of self-same predicates. Then back into the rhythm of lines balanced across the hemistich, accented by the internal rhyme of *enfer* and *centenaire*, before gliding across an enjambment into the unbroken march of the final line, which evokes the final line of "The Voyage" and of *Les Fleurs du Mal* itself: "Au fond de l'Inconnu pour trouver du *nouveau!*"[21] At the end of that poem the destination is at once unknown and known: the new. Here the end is unknown but the origin is known, and therefore not new: it is hell from which the infernal procession stems, and the stamp of this origin is the fraternal shiver it induces.

There is something *awful* about the synthesis of the subject, which can only be made manifest by its disjunction and by the surreal representation of this disjunction as image. What is awful is that we cannot evade the divisions of time upon which we rely for the synthesis that we are, disjoining and rejoining our unity at every instant. To reflect upon this too closely is to peer into the abyss, wherein one sees two prospects. One is the self-same repetition of minutes and of days. "What is the mysterious evil that gnaws at her athletic flanks," Baudelaire asks of a statue in "The Mask." He answers: "it is that tomorrow, alas! she must live again! / Tomorrow, the day after tomorrow and always! — like us!"[22] The other prospect one encounters is death, that division which Poe installs in the opening sentence of his tale: "Ye who read are still living; but I who write have shall have long since gone my way in the region of shadows."

---

21 FE, 454-455.

22 FE, 96-99: "Quel mal mystérieux ronge son flanc d'athlète? / .... C'est que demain, hélas! il faudra vivre encore! / Demain, après-demain et toujours! — comme nous!"

It is indeed the dead that we find in the central strophe of the central section of "The Seven Old Men," right after the evocation of the riddle of the sphinx, in the seventh of thirteen quatrains composing the poem:

> Dans la neige et la boue il allait s'empêtrant,
> Comme s'il écraisait des morts sous ses savates,
> Hostile à l'universe plutôt qu'indifferent.

—

> In snow and sludge he scuffled along,
> As if crushing the dead beneath worn out shoes,
> More hostile than indifferent to the universe.

At the stroke of noon, the hour of the shortest shadow, the dead that might otherwise speak through a shadow's voice are crushed beneath one's feet. But they are there just the same; they enter into the poem, breeding hostility where there might otherwise be indifference. As we see in the polemical excursions of his articles, Baudelaire feeds on such hostility; it nourishes his creative powers, such that flowers of evil may grow from what is crushed underfoot. The wintery, tainted hostility of the poem's central strophe is beautiful because it is antidote to indifference, and the dead flair up at the center of this poem as that which is different from the self-same, as the difference that lies *beneath* the procession of the same. "You tread upon the dead, Beauty," writes Baudelaire, and he follows this image with an avowal of indifference to the *origin* of that which displaces indifference:

> Que tu viennes du ciel ou de l'enfer, qu'importe,
> O Beauté! monstre énorme, effrayant, ingénu!
> Si ton œil, ton souris, ton pied, m'ouvrent la porte
> D'un Infini que j'aime et n'ai jamais connu?

—

> That you come from heaven or from hell, who cares,
> O Beauty! enormous, frightening, ingenuous monster!
> If your eye, your smile, your foot, opens the door
> Of an Infinite that I love and have never known![23]

Here it is a matter of indifference whether Beauty comes from Heaven or Hell, since what matters is that it opens *another* world, an Infinite beloved insofar as unknown. In "The Seven Old Men" we encounter an Infinite the speaker does *not* love and that he comes to know all too well, despite its uncanny aspect. The speaker undergoes an encounter with an unbearable infinity that he finds hideous rather than beautiful, but what is beautiful is the poem, the "frisson nouveaux"[24] that it creates, the Infinite it opens and makes thinkable through a disquieting tale.

As the speaker collapses in the face of the Infinite, horrified by the eternal air of decrepit repetition, we are given to think. He turns his back on the infernal procession, but we follow his retreat from the streets into a private chamber:

> Exaspéré comme un ivrogne qui voit double,
> Je rentrai, je fermai ma porte, épouvanté,
> Malade et morfondu, l'esprit fiévreux et trouble,
> Blessé par le mystère et par l'absurdité!
>
> Vainement ma raison voulait prendre la barre;
> La tempête en jouant déroutait ses efforts,
> Et mon âme dansait, dansait, vieille gabarre
> Sans mâts, sur une mer monstreuses et sans bords!

---

23 FE, 100-103.

24 Victor Hugo to Charles Baudelaire, 6 October 1859, in *Baudelaire: Un demi-siècle de lectures de Fleurs du mal (1855-1905)*, ed. André Guyaux (Paris: Presses de l'Université Paris-Sorbonne, 2007), 297.

Exasperated like a drunk who sees double,
I went home, I locked my door, terrified,
Sick and despondent, mind feverish and troubled,
Wounded by the mystery and absurdity!

Vainly my reason tried to take the helm;
The beguiling tempest baffling its efforts,
And my soul danced, danced, old barge
Without sails, upon a monstrous and unbounded sea!

"Vainly my reason tried to take the helm": what the speaker may not realize is that reason is itself the monstrous and unbounded sea by which his soul is tossed. For reason is, at once, the faculty of infinite regress and the faculty which tries to halt that regress by attaining the unconditioned, by thinking the absolute. Pushed beyond the bounds of possible experience by the immediate appearance of fractured synthesis, the subject of this impossible encounter finds himself cast outside the limits of understanding and "surrounded by a wide and stormy ocean, the true home of illusion, where many a fogbank and fast-melting icefloe tempts us to believe in new lands, while constantly deceiving the adventurous mariner with vain hopes, and involving him in adventures which he can never abandon and can never bring to an end."[25] This seems to be a sentence that Baudelaire had conceived and that Immanuel Kant had written seventy years before. Kant holds that reason must indeed take the helm upon the wide and stormy ocean that it also is: it can only hold in check its ungrounded pretensions to *know everything* through a discipline delimiting knowledge within the bounds of possible experience. Baudelaire's poem narrates the interruption of that capacity, the overthrowing of the bounds of sense through the dissolution of the imagination's synthetic faculty, which had enabled a seemingly harmonious integration of understanding and intuition. Shorn of synthesis, appearing to himself from the

25 Kant, CPR, A235-236/B295.

future and flickering into multiples without unity, the subject can only end up tossed upon the ocean of the unconditioned, the monstrous and unbounded sea of an absolute whose discipline he cannot master.

Baudelaire made a sketch of this unconditioned condition, which we find below the final strophe in one of the 1859 manuscripts of "Les Septs Vieillards" [Figure 2]. But Delacroix, *il miglior fabbro*, exhibited a more compelling version at the Salon of 1822 [Figure 3]. Baudelaire's speaker starts out in the swarming city full of dreams ("Je suivait") and he ends up in a locked chamber ("Je rentrai"), but the enclosure of that chamber gives way onto the underworld of Delacroix's *Dante and Virgil*. Unbalanced as Dante upon a barge without sails, the speaker has no Virgil beside him to offer a steadying hand. In Delacroix's Styx, as in the tones in the voice of Poe's SHADOW, it is the dead who rise from the depths. And as in Poe's tale, the dead of Delacroix's great canvas are *"connu et familiers."* According to the catalogue description for the 1822 Salon, "The damned cling to the barque or try to force their way onto it. Dante recognizes some Florentines among them."[26] It is the familiarity of the dead that shocks and horrifies, that makes them uncanny: their proximity, their *likeness*, like the boding and the memory of Evil, cannot be excluded.

In the noonday sun of Baudelaire's poem, the dead are trod underfoot. But how much time has passed since the appearance of the old man, as the speaker retreats to his chamber and as he undergoes his feverish sufferings? Seven hours may elapse unnoticed. Eventually the evening will come down, shadows will emerge, and the night will fall. Strange determinacies of number will give way to still more tenebrous indeterminacies, and one being, already wounded by an encounter with the multiplicity he is, may listen fearfully to the tones of a multitude of beings, those he will become, varying their cadences syllable by syllable. Meanwhile, we *do* have a Virgil to steady us: the poet or painter

26 Qtd. in Simon Lee, *Delacroix* (New York: Phaidon, 2015), 41.

FIGURE 2: Charles Baudelaire, "Les Sept Vieillards," Ms. C, Partial Reproduction *L'Atelier de Baudelaire,* ed. Claude Pichois and Jacques Dupont Vol. III (Paris: Honoré Champion, 2005), 2631

FIGURE 3: Eugène Delacroix, *Dante and Virgil (The Barque of Dante),* 1822

who composes mediations of impossible experience. We who are still among the living will find much to ponder among these alexandrines and quatrains poised at the fulcrum of Baudelaire's delicate touch, as we might while standing before the balanced storm of Delacroix's composition. There are seven figures rising from the River Styx. Is yet another about to appear? Who knows how many thousands and thousands, what multitudes, are just below the surface.

Knowledge of Nothing

The understanding, Kant tells us, is akin to an island "enclosed by nature itself within limits that can never be altered."[27] In the Transcendental Analytic, Kant surveys this domain in order to measure its extent and assign all its elements their proper place. He deduces the pure concepts of the understanding: the categories of quantity, quality, relation, and modality. He explores the syntheses of apprehension, reproduction, and recognition, held together by the transcendental unity of apperception. He theorizes the function of transcendental time determinations as mediating schemata. He enumerates the principles of pure understanding (rules for the objective use of the categories), including axioms of intuition, anticipations of perception, analogies of experience, and postulates of empirical thought in general. He takes special care to specify subdivisions of the analogies of experience: the principle of permanence (substance); the principle of succession (causality); the principle of simultaneity (interaction), showing how these function in accordance with the three categories of relation. There is nothing quite like this staggering exhibition of analytical precision, systematic rigor, and sheer conceptual originality in the history of philosophy. Above all, it amounts to a philosophy of *time* on an order of complexity that had never hitherto been imagined, let alone achieved. Taking stock of this achievement, Kant describes the island of the understanding as "the country of truth (a very charming name),"[28] and he prepares us for a more dangerous undertaking. We are now to set out on that wide and stormy ocean of reason we have likened above to the "monstrous and

27 Kant, CPR A235/B294-295.
28 Kant, CPR A235/B294-295.

unbounded sea" at the end of "The Seven Old Men" and to the tumultuous waters in the foreground and background of Delacroix's *Dante and Virgil*.

But just before departing the Transcendental Analytic in order to venture out to sea, Kant notes that he must "add something which, though in itself of no particular importance, may yet seem requisite for the completeness of the system."[29] This is his Table of the Division of the Concept of Nothing, the need for which Kant explains as follows:

> The highest concept from which all transcendental philosophy usually begins is the division into the possible and impossible. But, as all division presupposes a divided concept, a higher concept is required, and this is the concept of an object in general (taken as problematic, it being left undecided whether it be something or nothing). As the categories are only concepts which refer to things in general, the distinction whether an object is something or nothing must proceed according to the order and direction of the categories.[30]

Transcendental philosophy considers the conditions of all possible experience, and hence implicitly begins with the division of the possible and impossible. But the "higher concept" from which this division is drawn is that of "an object in general." The Table of Categories had laid out *a priori* concepts for the possible constitution of objects. Kant now applies the "order and direction of the categories" to a higher order analysis of the object in general as *nothing*, stipulating that "the corresponding division of the concept of 'something' follows automatically." This analysis is laid out in the table tacked on to the end of the Transcendental Analytic, a division of nothing added as something of no particular importance.[31]

29 Kant, CPR A290/B346.
30 Kant, CPR A290/B346.
31 Kant, CPR A292/B348.

Nothing as

1
Empty concept without an object,
ens rationis.

2
Empty object of a concept,
nihil privativum.

3
Empty intuition without an object,
ens imaginarium.

4
Empty object without a concept,
nihil negativum.

Kant might well have made more of his table, for it is not exactly trivial to have rescued the concept of nothing from pure indetermination through a division whose lucidity testifies to the power of Kant's Table of Categories, here subjected to a profound inversion. Crucially, there are four, rather than twelve, divisions of nothing because what is inverted are the divisions of the categories, the *heading* of each category (Quantity, Quality, Relation, Modality) rather than each concept falling under those headings. Let us outline these inversions by considering the Division of the Concept of Nothing according to the order and direction of the categories.

1. **Categories of Quantity: Totality, Plurality, Unity**
   "Opposed to the concepts of all, many, and one, there is the concept which cancels everything, that is, **none**." Kant defines the **empty concept without an object** as that of which no intuition can be found—which cannot be an object of *possible* experience, though it also cannot be counted as *impossible*. It is thus *ens rationis*, a being of reason. This the problematic concept of the noumena.

2. **Categories of Quality: Reality, Negation, Limitation**
Here "nothing" is an **empty object of a concept**, a privative remainder or negative relief considered *as* object. It requires an *indirect* concept, since it is drawn from "the absence of an object" (*nihil privativum*). Kant offers as examples "shadow or cold;" one might also consider the determinate hollow of a mould, where what is *not* there is understood through the lineaments of what is.

3. **Categories of Relation: Substance, Causality, Community**
An **empty intuition without an object** is "the mere form of intuition, without substance." This is the "merely formal condition of an object." As pure forms of intuition, space and time are not objects which are intuited, nor things which exist in themselves, but rather subjective conditions of sensibility that *cannot* be experienced, *ens imaginarium*.

4. **Categories of Modality: Possibility/Impossibility, Existence/Non-Existence, Necessity/Contingency**
An **empty object without a concept** is "the object of a concept which contradicts itself," such as a two-sided rectilinear figure. The object is empty (*nihil negativum*) because its concept is incoherent: its elements are stipulated but they are inconsistent with the constitution of an object of pure or empirical intuition.

In what follows we will be particularly concerned with #2 and #3: inversions of qualitative and relational categories, which Kant describes as "empty data for concepts." "It would be impossible," he tells us, "to represent to ourselves darkness, unless light had been given to the senses, or space, unless extended beings had been perceived. Negation [#2] as well as the mere form of intuition [#3] are, without something real, no objects."[32] What is interesting here is that Kant limns negative qualities and

32 Kant, CPR A292/B349.

pure forms from inversions of "something real;" he limns the negative traces of objects and the formal void of intuitions.

But what we must consider above all is a question Kant does not pursue. Kant has elaborated his Division of the Concept of Nothing according to the order and direction of the categories (pure concepts of the understanding). How then does the concept of nothing bear upon the movement from concepts of understanding to ideas of reason, which is pursued in the Transcendental Dialectic? What is the relation of *reason* to the concept of nothing? Pure reason, Kant stipulates, "does not concern itself with objects, it has no immediate relation to them and their intuition, but only to the understanding and its judgments."[33] Reason acts upon the conditioned knowledge of the understanding in order to push toward the unconditioned "whereby the unity of that knowledge is completed."[34] It thus produces what Kant calls *transcendental ideas*: concepts of the *totality* of conditions, of the absolute, for which the senses can produce no congruent object. Ideas are "concepts of pure reason insofar as they consider all empirical knowledge as determined by an absolute totality of conditions."[35] Although they overstep the bounds of possible experience, the production of ideas is a *necessary* activity of reason, which stems from the very nature of that faculty. The treatment of ideas as actual, as an *existing* totality, is a transcendental illusion, born of mistaking subjective concepts for real things. But it is "a demand of reason"[36] that a series of conditions be pushed to the point of the unconditioned, considered as an absolute totality, such that reason is necessarily prone to the illusion of hypostatizing concepts of totality as real totalities.

.

33 Kant, CPR A306/B363.
34 Kant, CPR A307/B364.
35 Kant, CPR A327/B384.
36 Kant, CPR A332/B389.

It is the categories of relation, under the third division of Kant's table, from which the three ideas of reason—Soul, World, and God—are generated by the activity of reason. The categories of relation, in Kant's transcendental logic, correspond with the three types of syllogism in general logic: categorical, hypothetical, and disjunctive. It is the inferential activity of reason upon concepts of relation (substance, cause, community) through these three syllogisms that produces the transcendental ideas. Kant explains:

> We will find as many pure concepts of reason [Ideas] as there are kinds of relations, which the understanding represents to itself by means of the categories; and we will have to look for an **unconditioned**, firstly, of the **categorical** synthesis in a subject; secondly, of the **hypothetical** synthesis of the members of a series; thirdly, of the **disjunctive** synthesis of the parts of a system.[37]

The absolute unity of the thinking subject is the idea of Soul; the absolute unity of the series of conditions of appearance is the idea of World; the absolute unity of the condition of all objects of thought in general is the idea of God. These correspond to the categories of relation: the idea of Soul treats the unity of the thinking subject as *substance*; the idea of World treats the unity of conditioned appearances as a totality of *causes*; the idea of God treats the unity of all objects of thought as absolute *community* or *interrelation*, the being of all beings. These three ideas also correspond to three kinds of knowledge: psychology (Soul); cosmology (World); theology (God). And while Kant *deduces* his table of categories according to what must be the case in order for our experience to be as it is, he *derives* the ideas from the inferential activity of reason directly upon the three concepts of relation.

---

37 Kant, CPR, A323/B379.

Now, in his Table of the Division of the Concept of Nothing, Kant deduces an obverse of the concepts of relation under heading #3: the concept of nothing as empty intuition without an object, the pure *form* of intuition, without substance, such as pure space and pure time. Our question is: can we derive an idea of reason from this inversion of the categories of relation? Here we must proceed carefully. The derivation of the ideas from concepts depends upon syntheses of conditions drawn from inferences through the three syllogisms (categorical, hypothetical, disjunctive), which correspond to each category of relation. But here we are dealing with a concept of nothing situated at the level of the *heading* of the category of relation, rather than each concept under the category. Moreover, there is literally *nothing* for reason to pursue through a series of conditions toward the unconditioned: there is no subject, there are no members of a series, no parts of a system to push toward an absolute unity and synthesize as a totality.

However, we may still be prone to a transcendental illusion incumbent upon reason's treatment of this concept of nothing (the absence of relation *per se*) as an absolute, as a totality, as an *objective* unity of nothing rather than a *subjective* form of empty determination. Why? What is the demand of reason at work here, since there is no series of conditions to pursue? The demand is already implicit in the very act of conceptualizing mere form *as nothing*, of treating empty intuition without an object as a *concept*. The understanding derives a concept of nothing from the emptiness of intuition, but thought *as a concept of* nothing, empty intuition is not empty *intuition*, but emptiness as such. The concept of nothing *unifies* and *abstracts* emptiness, and this is the implication of concept formation to which reason responds in all cases: because it *only* relates to concepts and not to objects formed by synthesis, it relates to the unities determined by concepts as if they were things in themselves (the unity of subject, the unity of causality, the unity of beings, the unity of nothing). Kant will tell us later, in his discussion of the Transcendental

Ideal, that "no one can determinately think a negation, unless he founds it on the opposed affirmation."[38] But the concept of nothing (rather than the logical function of negation, which is already included among the categories) implies a vocation to think negation as determinate—to think formal emptiness as nothing—for it is the function of concepts to determine that which they are concepts *of*. Reason grasps this implication of the concept, and strains to think the concept in itself. This would be the transcendental idea of nothing, of *emptiness in itself*: the idea of absolute emptiness is the Void. As in the case of the other ideas (though here more paradoxically), reason would treat the concept of nothing as a thing, as the absolute unity of nothingness, the existing totality of non-existence.

We have taken up this problem because the aspiration to think the Void, and to situate it within a moral universe that it threatens with incoherence, is of central importance within *Les Fleurs du Mal*. The pursuit of the Void as a regulative idea is expressed with perfect rigor in a tercet of "Obsession" that demarcates one of the metaphysical limits of Baudelaire's book:

> Comme tu me plairais, ô nuit! sans ces étoiles
> Dont la lumière parle un langage connu!
> Car je cherche le vide, et le noir, et le nu!
>
> —
>
> How you would please me, o night! without these stars
> Whose light speaks a language we know!
> For I seek the void, and the black, and the bare![39]

Knowledge of objects—relational knowledge of the language of the stars—does not suffice to meet the desire of the speaker. He seeks the absolutization of emptiness, figured first as the subtraction of the stars from the night and then objectified as

38 Kant, CPR A575/B603.
39 FE, 262-263.

a vacant totality: "le vide, et le noir, et le nu!" The attainment of such an absolute would seal an impossible compact between subjective and objective emptiness. And this compact would be pleasing, since it would offer an objective correlate of the emptiness of the mere form of intuition. It would totalize the restless nothingness of the subject implicit in its bare capacity for receptivity, its *need* for givenness.

But such pleasure would come at a price. For how can we situate the desire to think the Void as an idea, as an absolute, in relation to the ideas of Soul, World, and God? The problem is that of the *harmony* of ideas: of their regulative convergence upon a unity of totalities. The ideas "are sophistries not of human beings but of pure reason itself,"[40] Kant tells us. But despite the uncanny resonance of this striking formulation, Soul, World, and God are comforting sophistries. If we achieve a discipline of reason that holds it to a regulative rather than constitutive use, it will direct the understanding "to a certain aim, towards which the directional lines of all its rules converge in one point."[41] This one point is "the systematic unity of the knowledge of the understanding,"[42] which is approached though a *hypothetical* use of pure reason. We proceed *as if* psychological, cosmological, and theological totalities were objective unities. Such a hypothetical use of reason constitutes a "procedure by which the empirical and determinate use of the understanding can reach thoroughgoing harmony with itself."[43] As *maxims* of pure reason, the sophistries of reason do not lead to conflicting ideas but rather to "one single interest": the thoroughgoing unity of knowledge.

Moreover, reason achieves moral reassurance through the harmony of regulative ideas insofar as they converge upon "the

40 Kant, CPR A339/B397.
41 Kant, CPR A644/B672.
42 Kant, CPR A647/B675.
43 Kant, CPR A666/B694.

ideal of the highest good." In order for a moral world to be *intelligible*, Kant argues, our hope for happiness must be rationally connected with the moral endeavor to make oneself *worthy* of happiness. But there is nothing in the natural world, nothing in experience, that would assure us of this connection:

> With mere nature as our ground, therefore, the necessary connection of a hope for happiness with the unceasing endeavor of rendering oneself worthy of happiness cannot be known by reason; rather, it can only be hoped for if a **highest reason**, which rules according to moral laws, is accepted at the same time as underlying nature as its cause.[44]

The idea of such a highest reason as the author of both natural and moral laws unites Soul, World, and God insofar as it draws nature and freedom into rational unity with the good. The regulative harmony of ideas is thus essential to morality as well as to the unity of knowledge.

> The idea of such an intelligence in which the most perfect moral will, united with the highest blessedness, is the cause of all happiness in the world, as far as this happiness corresponds exactly with one's morality, that is, the worthiness to be happy, I call the **ideal of the highest good**. It is, therefore, only in the ideal of the highest **original** good that pure reason can find the ground of the practically necessary connection of both elements of the highest derivative good, namely, the ground of an intelligible, that is, **moral** world.[45]

The moral world is an intelligible world because it is one that *makes sense* of "a system of self-rewarding morality," which is only an idea. It is an idea that makes sense according to the premise that Soul, World, and God may be united through the

44 Kant, CPR A810/B838.
45 Kant, CPR A810/B838.

ideal of the highest good, whereby what *is* the case converges with what *ought* to be the case if we strive to be worthy of our agency as rational beings.

Now, even considered in its regulative rather than constitutive use, the idea of the Void does not converge upon a single point with those of Soul, World, and God. For to think the Void as an absolute one would have to think the extinction of every Soul, the annihilation of the World, and the death of God. The price of the pleasure of the Void would be the cancellation of all capacity for pleasure. The reluctant inclination toward this idea, and the logical requirement of oblivion it entails, is what Baudelaire calls "Le Goût du Néant." But even if it is impossible to think the Void (*cogito, ergo sum*), the desire to do so stems from the relation of reason to the concept of nothing (rather than mere negation). It is a sophistry *of reason*, but one whose regulative discipline instills no comfort. The Void cannot subsume the other three ideas any more than they can subsume the Void, because they must *each* be thought as absolute, so even the inclination to think this idea produces a dissonance within the regulative use of reason.

Insofar as the poet of *Les Fleurs du Mal* pledges his determination to "seek the void, and the black, and the bare," we must understand that the book does not simply construct a conflict between "Spleen" and "Ideal," as if these were two discrete principles expressing a duality of human nature or a clash of discrepant moods. There is disharmony *within* the Ideal. The Ideal is self-contradictory, since to seek the Void is to seek the elimination of all that could find it. And the pursuit of the Void disrupts the ideal of the highest good by rendering the unity it requires unintelligible. The regulative activity of reason no longer converges upon a single point: since the ideas of Soul, World, and God are just as ineliminable as the Void, it is impossible to think their harmony through to the end. The Void is malicious: it infects the Ideal. There is Spleen because of this infection, but the infection is endemic to the Ideal itself.

Here is the poem titled "Ideal" in *Les Fleurs du Mal*:

Ce ne seront jamais ces beautés de vignettes,
Produit avariés, nés d'un siècle vaurien,
Ces pieds à brodequins, ces doigts à castagnettes,
Qui sauront satisfaire un coeur comme le mien.

Je laise à Gavarni, poète des cloroses,
Son troupeau gazouillant de beautés d'hopitâl,
Car je ne puis ne trouver parmi ces pâles roses
Une fleur qui ressemble à mon rouge idéal.

Ce qu'il fait à ce coeur profond comme un abîme,
C'est vous, Lady Macbeth, âme puissante au crime,
Rêve d'Eschyle éclose au climat des autans;

Ou bien toi, grande Nuit, fille de Michel-Ange,
Qui tors paisiblement dans une pose étrange
Tes appas façonnés au bouches des Titans!

—

Never will these beauties in vignettes,
Debased products, born of a miscreant century,
These feet in buskins, these fingers in castanets,
Know how to satisfy a heart like mine.

I leave to Gavarni, poet of chlorosis,
His chirping flock of hospital belles,
For I cannot find among such pale roses
One flower resembling my ideal red.

Profound as an abyss, what this heart requires
Is you, Lady Macbeth, soul equal to the crime,
Dream of Aeschylus hatched in storm winds;

Or you, great Night, Michelangelo's daughter,
Who peacefully twists in exotic pose
Your charms fashioned in the mouths of Titans! [46]

The violence of this sonnet lies in the bracing shift of registers at the volta: with the evocation of an ideal red, we break from parodic ridicule of "beauties in vignettes"—the hollowing out of the romantic ideal by the pale representations of "un siècle vaurien"—to a thunderous affirmation of literary and mythic figures of an ideal worthy of the absolute, drawn from the Renaissance and its inheritance of antiquity. In "Evening Harmony," Baudelaire evokes "Un coeur tendre, qui hait le néant vaste et noir!"[47] ("A tender heart, which hates the vast and black nothing!"), but that is not "a heart like mine." What we see in "Ideal" is that the heart which aspires toward the regulative idea of "the void, and the black, and the bare" aligns itself with evil, rather than with the ideal of the highest good: a heart profound as an abyss demands a soul equal to the crime. The final tercet then hails another counterpart of the abyssal heart in the figure of "great Night" sculpted by Michelangelo and fashioned, allegorically, by Titans. The dream of Aeschylus—the birth of tragedy in Clytemnestra's crime, relayed by Lady Macbeth and akin to Night itself—hatches a deviation of the absolute from the pallid ideals of the supposedly righteous. It is this deviation, this deviousness *within* the Ideal, to which the heart must be adequate insofar as it inclines toward the Void, insofar as it is profound as an abyss.

Were this poem all that remained of *Les Fleurs du Mal*, we could imagine how Baudelaire might regard Kant's ideal of the highest good. But the psychological proclivities of individual philosophers and poets are far from the point. The question is whether there is a rational *implication* of the concept of nothing—though "of no particular importance" to Kant himself—that

[46] FE, 92-93.
[47] FE, 178-179.

might lead one to pursue it as an absolute. This might require a heart profound as an abyss, but that would not reduce such a pursuit to pathology. Rather, it would signal the determination to pursue the Ideal in the element of its dissonance, to brave the discord of a *logical revolt* that would be generative of "new flowers,"[48] of an "ideal red" both beautiful and fatal: *ces fleurs maladives*.[49] Such an endeavor would be a symptom, but not of a human being. It would be a symptom of reason itself.

Indeed, the pursuit of the idea of the Void would not only be a sophistry of reason to be kept in check by discipline, but an *irony* of reason infiltrating its regulative use. This is the rational sense in which we could read the question, posed with characteristic precision, in "Heuton Timoroumenos":

> Ne suis-je pas un faux accord
> Dans la divine symphonie,
> Grace à la vorace Ironie
> Qui me secoue et qui me mord?
>
> —
>
> Am I not a false chord
> In the divine symphony,
> Thanks to the voracious Irony
> That shakes me and sinks in its teeth?[50]

The regulative harmony of the ideas proceeds *as if* a divine symphony brought Soul, World, and God into alignment, unifying freedom with nature and securing the intelligibility of morality. But the false chord that shakes this divine symphony stems from the same source as the capacity to think it—the "I"—and the voracious Irony of this disruption is that it is proper to reason

---

48 FE, 76-77.
49 FE, 42-43.
50 FE, 270-273.

itself. I am the source of the discord, but it is *as if* it is exterior to me, such that I fall prey to it. Not only the imagination but also reason may take up the allegorical function of objectifying concepts, relating to them as if they really existed. But when the concept of nothing itself turns back upon the subject from which it stems, exteriorized as the idea of the Void, it shakes us and sinks in its teeth.

If it is salvation that is promised by the ideal of the highest good, it is damnation that follows from seeking the Void. There is a word for the deviations it installs within the harmony of ideas: Evil. And there is a *figure* of those deviations, of their irony, of the irony of figuring the Void: Satan. While the poems of "Revolt" in Les Fleurs du Mal still seem to many the mere caprice of an *enfant terrible*,[51] we regard such judgments as beside the point—since one might draw from Kant's analysis of the concept of nothing a transcendental derivation of Romantic Satanism, which finds the point of its highest lucidity in Baudelaire's work. Let us see how Baudelaire pursues the paradoxes, the ironies, and the figural impasses this entails. No one has ever done so with such determination and despair—a Luciferian determination to which Kant's soul did not aspire to be equal. Nor did Kant have the means to do so, for what is at stake is the relation of reason to *poetic* determination.

* * *

The poetic problem with the pursuit of the void is that it has to be *figured*.[52] This is not quite as difficult a problem for ideas of

---

51 For a summary and critique of such reductions of Baudelaire's romantic Satanism, see Jonathan Culler, "Baudelaire's Satanic Verses," *diacritics* 28.3: 86-100.

52 In the previous section I capitalize Void in order to emphasize the conceptual framework in which it supplements Kantian ideas of Soul, World, and God. Hereafter I primarily write the word in lowercase, as I work through the relevance of this conceptual reconstruction to Baudelaire's oeuvre.

Soul, World, and God, which are indeed figures of the absolute, since they are ideas of a positive totality: the permanence of psychological unity, the totality of a causal series, the being of all beings. But the emptiness of all? To represent this idea is to represent it *as a being*, to bring it into relation with other representations, to cognize emptiness without an object as an object. We see this problem in Baudelaire's figure of a night without stars in "Obsession"—this is a subtractive representation, operating on the level of the concept, *nihil privativum*, rather than on the level of the absolute. Or we see it in the allegorical mode of "great Night," the peaceful twist and exotic pose of Michelangelo's sculpture. To allegorize the void is to negate the void itself, to twist it into *something*. Such is the impasse of poiesis, of *making*, when confronted with the desire for absolute nothingness. If the void cannot be thought without eliminating the thinker, it cannot be figured without eliminating the void.

This impasse of figuration will be addressed by the recognition and incorporation of its voracious Irony, such that the registration of irony must accompany the *material inscription* of the void (writing) and the *images* of the void produced in intuition (reading). "L'Irrémédiable" performs a stepwise mediation of this irony.

> Une Idée, une Forme, un Être
> Parti de l'azure et tombé
> Dans un Styx bourbeaux et plombé
> Où nul oeil du Ciel ne pénètre;
>
> —
>
> An Idea, a Form, a Being
> Parted the azure and fell
> In a murky and leaden Styx
> Where no eye of Heaven penetrates;[53]

53 FE, 274-277.

The first line of the poem is a summa of our argument: "An Idea, a Form, a Being" encapsulates the relation between absolute emptiness (idea of void), empty intuition (concept of nothing), and figural objectification (poiesis) that constitute the representational problem of evil in *Les Fleurs du Mal*. The intervention of the void as an Idea, drawn from a Form, now descends the ladder of its genesis, figured as a Being that "Parted the azure and fell"—an eruption of emptiness that splits the unity of God and World and falls into a region inaccessible to the eye of Heaven. The void intervenes in the harmony of ideas like a wedge of nothingness that divides the being of all beings, falls into the world, and lodges in the Soul as its invisible damnation.

The effect upon the soul of this fall is described in "Destruction":

Sans cesse à mes côtés s'agite le Démon;
Il nage autour de moi comme un air impalpable;
Je l'avale et le sense qui brûle mon poumon
Et l'emplit d'un désire éternel et coupable.

Parfois il prend, sachant mon grand amour de l'Art,
La forme de la plus séduisante des femmes,
Et, sous de spécieux prétextes de cafard,
Accoutumne ma lèvre à des philtres infâmes.

Il me conduit ainsi, loin de regard de Dieu,
Haletant et brisé de fatigue, au milieu
Des plaines de l'Ennui, profondes et désertes,

Et jette dan mes yeux pleins de confusion
Des vêtements souillés, des blessures ouvertes,
Et l'appareil sanglant de la Destruction!

—

> Ceaselessly the Demon flickers at my side;
> He swims around me as impalpable air;
> I breathe him in and feel him burn my lungs
> And suffuse them with eternal and guilty desire.
>
> Sometimes he takes, knowing my great love of Art,
> The form of the most seductive woman,
> And, under specious pretext of malaise,
> Accustoms my lip to infamous philters.
>
> He leads me thus, far from the gaze of God,
> Panting and broken with fatigue, amid
> The plains of Ennui, deep and deserted,
>
> And casts before my eyes full of confusion
> Soiled garments, open wounds,
> And the bloody weapons of Destruction![54]

Ennui is allegorized as an affective correlate of the void: "The plains of Ennui, deserted and profound." It is "The Demon," figural mediator, who leads the speaker to these empty plains, "far from the gaze of God," just as the Devil of "L'Irrémédiable" plunges into "a murky and leaden Styx / Where no eye of Heaven penetrates." Here one becomes *invisible* to God and *blind* to the ideal of the highest good. Thus, "bloody weapons of Destruction" are cast before the speaker's eyes. Both Soul and God are rendered sightless in the desert or the fathomless depths of the World, which render its unity indeterminate. But just as the void is blinding, so too does it invade the terrain of the aesthetic: the Demon who personifies its emptiness deploys the seduction of appearances to deceive, and deception itself—its specious pretexts—doubles the pursuit of truth with infamous pleasures to which we become accustomed. Such an account is close to Kant's description of the sophistries of reason, but while

[54] FE, 368-369.

Kant teaches us to tame those sophistries through the discipline of reason, even the *regulative* pursuit of the void is a form of seduction leading to Destruction.

Baudelaire registers that the void *has to be thought*. "Ceaselessly the Demon flickers at my side": the void is an omnipresent emptiness, an impalpable air at once exterior to and interiorized by the subject, which fills one with "eternal and guilty desire." To seek the void, and the black, and the bare is to incur the guilt of thinking. It is an eternal desire because it is a pursuit of the absolute, and thus unrealizable for a finite being. We are guilty twice over: because we think an absolute misaligned with the ideal of the highest good, and because we cannot attain the absolute that we think. Even to represent our effort to think it is to represent emptiness as a being, the Demon. Its very presence, ineradicable, makes manifest the failure that it is, that we are.

In "L'Irrémédiable" the irony of such guilt is made explicit. We are led through a series of "spotless emblems, perfect tableaux" of the alignment of the Devil with the void.

> Un Ange, imprudent voyageur
> Qu'a tenté l'amour de difform,
> A fond d'un cauchemar énorme
> Se débattant comme un nageur,
>
> —
>
> An Angel, imprudent voyager
> Lured by love of disform,
> To the depth of an enormous nightmare
> Floundering like a swimmer,

An Angel in love with disform, the Being that parts the azure struggles against a gigantic whirlpool and descends without a lamp down stairs without a rail into a dank depth

Où veillent des monstres visqueux
Dont les larges yeux de phosphore
Font une nuit plus noire encore
Et ne rendent visibles qu'eux;

—

Where viscous monsters keep watch
Whose wide eyes of phosphorous
Blacken even the night
And make visible only themselves;

That these emblems of "an irremediable fortune" are "spotless" and "perfect" just goes to show, the poem quips, "that the Devil / Is good at whatever he does!" The Devil is perfect at imperfection—hence his dialectical sophistication. The irony of his emblems is that, as particulars, they imperfectly render the *absolute* imperfection from which he stems (they cancel the void by representing it) and their imperfection thus makes them perfect emblems of imperfection. The recognition and the riddling of irony recuperates the misprision of representing nothing, for irony is nothing but the truth of misprision.

The poem thus concludes with two strophes reflecting upon the duplicity of the soul, its doubling, introduced by such irony:

Tête-à-tête sombre et limpide
Qu'un coeur devenu son miroir!
Puits de Vérité, clair et noir,
Où tremble une étoile livide,

Un phare ironique, infernal,
Flambeau des grâces sataniques,
Soulagement et gloire uniques,
— La conscience dans le Mal!

—

> Somber and limpid tête-à-tête
> Of a heart become its own mirror!
> Well of Truth, clear and black
> Where trembles a livid star,
>
> An ironic beacon, infernal,
> Torch of satanic graces,
> Singular glory and solace,
> — The conscience within Evil.

The void of a doubled heart—split by "An Idea, a Form, a Being" at variance with the harmony of ideas—is figured as a "Well of Truth, clear and black / Where trembles a livid star." This heart is a well of *Truth* because it knows the truth of irony: the unattainable absolute of a night without stars (the erasure of familiar knowledge) is replaced by a clear and black surface reflecting *one* star: Lucifer as figure of the void. This star is indeed an "*ironic* beacon," since it represents the presentation of the void as image and figure, which it is not. Such an ironic beacon, doubling the figure of the Devil within the interiority of the subject, is the adequate figure of "The conscience within Evil." The irony of conscience is *within* Evil, since the problem of the relation between Good and Evil stems from the division of the Ideal, introducing an opposition that is asymmetrical insofar as Evil is already inherent to the division itself. Lucifer's star is the ironic beacon of the constitutive division that conscience *is*. To recognize the radicality of this irony—to think it as irremediable—is to think it as a misalignment at the level of the ideas, as a discord within the divine symphony rather than a mere privation, rather than a mere *failure* to live up to the discipline of the moral law. This is the irony of an idea that divides the ideal, but the reflexive irony this entails is one of representation: the irony of having to figure objectlessness as object. Combining these two levels, we grasp the irony of misprision recognized as Truth: the irony that only imperfection is perfect, since perfection is imperfect.

Such *absolute* irony issues from the void, and it is Irremediable (a "voracious Irony"), because it is the irony of an absolute that divides the absolute. The desire to think it stems from knowledge of nothing, which is *a priori* knowledge of the division of its concept: the determination of the concept of nothing, rather than its reduction to pure indetermination.

We can thus elaborate an ironic dialectic of determination operative at two levels in Baudelaire's "Satanism." First, there is an ironic identity of freedom and damnation, of which the fallen angel is the traditional emblem. To be determin*ing* is to be determin*ed*: that is the dialectic of determination the Luciferian figure represents. This problem derives from the splitting of the ideal, skewing the unity of Soul, World, and God such that the orientation of freedom toward the ideal of the highest good is disoriented. The Luciferian figure grasps and acts upon this disorientation, instantiating evil as logical revolt and emblematizing the freedom to think as the descent of damnation. Second, as figure of the void—("An Idea, a Form, a *Being*")—the Devil situates the first problem of determination (freedom/damnation) in relation to a second problem of determination, which operates at the level of signification. To grasp the relation between these two levels of the problem in *Les Fleurs du Mal*, one must understand how they constitute, together, the problem of *poetic* determination.

We see the genesis of this problem in one of Baudelaire's earliest poems, collected among his juvenilia:

> Il est de chastes mots que nous profanons tous;
> Les amoureux d'encens font un abus étrange.
> Je n'en connais pas un qui n'*adore* quelque *ange*
> Dont ceux du Paradis sont, je crois, peu jaloux.
>
> On ne doit accorder ce nom sublime et doux
> Qu'à de beaux coeurs bien purs, vierges et sans mélange.
> Regardez! il lui pend à l'aile quelque fange

Quand votre *ange* en riant s'assied sur vos genoux.

J'eus, quand j'étais enfant, ma naïve folie
— Certaine fille aussi mauvaise que jolie —
Je l'appelais *mon ange*. Elle avait cinq galants.

Pauvres fous! nous avons tant soif qu'on nous caresse
Que je voudrais encor tenir quelque drôlesse
À qui dire: *mon ange* — entre deux draps bien blancs.[55]

—

There are some chaste words we all profane;
Lovers of incense make a strange misuse.
I don't know a soul who doesn't *adore* some *angel*
Of whom those in Paradise are, I think, not too jealous.

One may accord that sublime and sweet name
Only to those beautiful hearts truly pure, virgin and unmixed.
Look! some filth gets on the wing
When your smiling *angel* sits upon your knee.

I had, as a child, my youthful folly
— A certain girl as naughty as pretty —
I would call *my angel*. She had five suitors.

Poor fools! We so crave a caress
That I would still cling to some floozy
To call: *my angel* — between two clean white sheets.

---

[55] Charles Baudelaire, Oeuvres Complètes I, 202-203. My translation. The manuscript of the poem is available with a transcription in Claude Pichois and Jacques Dupont, eds., *L'Atelier de Baudelaire: Les Fleurs du Mal*, Éditions diplomatique IV (Paris: Honoré Champion, 2005), 3486-3487. The poem was included in a letter to Baudelaire's brother dated December 31, 1840.

An angel is a figurative mediation of the ideal, and the poem diagnoses the misuse of such figures to idealize the mundane. More specifically, it diagnoses the misuse of *words* in such idealizations. *Ange* is a "chaste word," properly accorded only to hearts that are "truly pure, virgin, and unmixed." It is profaned by its deployment for erotic pursuits, since those *to whom* it is applied are unworthy of it, unequal to Angels of Paradise. As soon as the idealization *works*, drawing the suitor's "angel" onto his knee, it is unworked: some filth gets on the wing.

But here the poem is more clever than its speaker. The speaker would reserve the use of chaste words for adequate referents: those pure, virgin, and unmixed hearts that measure up to angels of Paradise. Thus he means to satirize those to whom the term is applied ("quelque drôlesse") as well as those who improperly apply it, including himself ("Pauvres fous!"). But the poem's emphasis upon the materiality of the signifier draws our attention to the inherent impurity of the word, the context of its articulation and its mundane inscription, which suggests that it *cannot* address the pure, the virgin, and the unmixed without contaminating the referent. Whenever the signifier is applied to the ideal, some filth gets on the wing. The implicit recognition of this irony is inscribed in the poem's final line, where the speaker imagines addressing "quelque drôlesse" as "*mon ange*" between two clean white sheets. The imagined scene plays upon the concupiscent hypocrisy of erotic idealization, but the *inscription* of the scene plays upon the writing of signifiers in ink between white pages. Meaning itself is idealization; its sublimating activity is impeded by the persistent materiality of the signifier.

However, there is one angel to whom such imperfect idealization is perfectly applied, since he embodies its irony: Satan. Put otherwise, the materiality of the signifier is the switching point where one may change tracks in pursuit of the Ideal. If the impurity of reference compromises the mediating unity of Soul, World, and God, such impurity finds a referent adequate to its imperfection in the Devil. It is as if this early poem of Baudelaire's contains an apology for conversion to the Devil's party, through the implicit realization of the signifier's incapacity to signify the ideal: one will have to make a virtue of necessity by embracing this misfortune. But another obstacle lies in wait: the pursuit of an obverse ideal still leads toward the absolute along a reverse path—from Being, to Form, to Idea—and the Idea itself still cannot be adequately represented by its figure, however ingeniously we incorporate the irony of this fact. The *emptiness* of the absolute (Void) is just as compromised by reference as its *plenitude* (God)—perhaps even more so, since the being of beings may include all the beings within it, while the void must expel them from its essence. Pure nothingness is inhospitable even to that irony which approaches it; nothingness may be that *from which* duplicity derives, but it does not itself include it. If the signifier interrupts the purity of clean white sheets with its inky residue, then one would have to black out the whole page to signify the void. There could be no differentiation of signifiers, just as there could be no stars in the sky.

One should not back away from thinking through the blackness of the signifier (the relation of black signifier to white page) in terms of race—or, rather, in terms of the agency of racializing imagination within the figural world of Baudelaire's poems. Implicitly recognizing that the "unmixed" *whiteness* of Paradisal angels and blank pages ("sans mélange" "entre deux draps bien blancs") is interrupted by the *blackness* of signifiers through which they would be addressed in writing, the poems will pursue erotic and idealizing representations of angels that are indeed of mixed race. Figures of the idealized creole and of the fallen mulatto mistress in *Les Fleurs du Mal* can be understood not only in terms of the exoticizing proclivities of its author but also in terms of a metaphysical and representational problem to which these figures provide a vexed solution. The colonies offer the nineteenth century European male poet an opportunity to fasten the irony of the signifier to a figure of the angel that may be idealized as *mélange*, while the figural blackness of the obedient slave figures the longed-for submission of the void.

These are the representational solutions pursued in "To a Creole Lady" through a series of tropes as poetically wooden as they are ideologically significant. The "unknown charms" of the poem's addressee suggest a path less trodden toward the ideal, though it remains well-worn. Described as a "brown enchantress" of noble bearing ("A dans le cou des airs noblement maniérés"), the hypothetical effect of the Creole Lady's arrival in France is imagined in the sonnet's final tercet as a conquest of the European ideal:

> Vous feriez, à l'abri des ombreuses retraites,
> Germer mille sonnets dans le coeur des poètes,
> Que vos grands yeux rendraient plus soumis que vos noirs.
>
> —
>
> You would, within an arbor of reclusive shadows,
> Germinate a thousand sonnets in the heart of the poets
> Whom your wide eyes would make more submissive than
>   your blacks.[56]

Here the black slave serves as the archetype of submission exceeded by the devotion of white poets to the mediating figure between African colonies and European culture: the creole gentlewoman whose pale and warm hue ("Son teint est pâle et chaud") draws the light and darkness of opposing absolutes into an arbor of reclusive shadows. That this is a terrible poem—tipping over from the saccharine caution of a missive sent to a revered woman's husband into the vulgarity of bland colonial reassurance—should not be reduced to a symptom of Baudelaire's youth at the time of its composition. Rather, the casual deployment of "vos noirs" to parallel the romantic submission of French poets to a creole slaveholder expresses a metaphysical disavowal analyzed by Lewis Gordon in terms of

---

56 FE, 224-225.

bad faith.⁵⁷ "Vos noirs" are those ideologically posited figures of the void whose submission, supposedly, can be counted upon—though the poem cannot elide the implication that they may be *less* submissive than Frenchmen conquered by the wide eyes of a Creole Lady. European submission to this figure of colonial mediation is predicated upon the submission of blackness to *poetic* mediation: the inclusion of "vos noirs" serves to fill out a rhyme with "gloire" and "Loire." In "The Previous Life," it is the "naked slaves" fanning the speaker's brow "whose only care was to fathom / The dolorous secret of my languor."⁵⁸ As the metaphor suggests ("approfondir"), that *secret douloureux* involves a sorrowful orientation toward the void, subsumed into a life of calm pleasures ("C'est là que j'ai vécu dans les voluptés calmes") by the imagined servitude of slaves. And even if the reference were to ancient rather than modern slavery, those slaves are also merged with the modern referent of "À Une Dame Créole" within the overall context of the volume. This is the crux of blackness and nothingness that figures in the psyche of Europe as a kind of metaphysical threat that must be conquered or sublimated. We can approach it through the problem of poetic determination constructed by Baudelaire's interrogation of the word *ange*: since the black signifier cannot signify the pure white ideal without besmirching it, it will have to take a mediating path. The ideal will be routed through an arbor of reclusive shadows where a brown enchantress can enfold the ironic materiality of reference and make it glow with a pale and warm hue. Such would be the comforting solution of the *mélange*.

Yet this comfort will not survive within the crucible of actual eros. We change tracks in pursuit of the ideal at the switching point of the signifier: with the fall of an Idea, a Form, a Being

---

57 Lewis R. Gordon, *Bad Faith and Antiblack Racism* (Amherst: Humanity Books, 1995). See also Christopher Miller, *Blank Darkness: Africanist Discourse in French* (Chicago: University of Chicago Press, 1985).

58 FE, 80-81.

(void as fallen angel) installing a disharmony of the ideal, we descend *from* thwarted ascension toward the angelic unity of Soul, World, and God *to* the signifier in black ink on white sheets, and from there toward the figure of a mistress both dark and pale. In "Les Promesses d'un Visage,"[59] a "pale beauty" is lauded for black hair, black eyes, and black eyebrows from which shadows seem to flow ("D'où semblent couler des ténèbres"), and these are followed down beneath a smooth and dark ("bistré") belly to a rich fleece ("Une riche toison") that is equal in density to a Night without stars ("Nuit sans étoiles, Nuit obscure!"). Here the absolute void to which the speaker of "Obsession" aspires is found in the loins of a tenebrous mistress. But the soothing mediation of referential irony afforded by this complex of racial and sexual figuration meets its impasse precisely as it achieves its goal: it will merge with the fallen angel from which the irony of the signifier descends, the Devil.

In "The Jewels," the erotic advance of the dark mistress ("ce teint fauve et brun") is described as "more coaxing than malicious Angels" ("plus câlins que les Anges du mal").[60] The same black eyes that promise erotic fulfillment become sources of hellfire, and in "Lethe" "the abyss of your bed" comes to figure the satanic identity of freedom and damnation:

À mon destin, désormais mon délice,
J'obéirai comme un prédestiné;
Martyr docile, innocent condamné,
Dont la ferveur attise le supplice,

—

My destiny, hereafter my delight,
I shall obey as a predestination;
Docile martyr, condemned innocent,
Whose fervor fuels the ordeal,[61]

59 Baudelaire, *Oeuvres Complètes* I, 163.
60 FE, 104-107.
61 FE, 134-135.

We have come full circle, from the fall of an Idea, a Form, a Being that divides the azure, down to the contamination of the absolute by the signifier, through the renunciation of the *ange sans mélange* for the *mal ange mélangé*, and thus back to the incarnation of the void as the Being of the fall: the fate of figural contradiction. The irony of the solution is that in order for it to work, the figure that would remediate the irremediable inaccessibility of the void will have to merge with the figure of Satan to do so, and the Devil is good at whatever he does: he is the destroyer of perfect solutions. Salvation will amount to damnation. This inescapable contradiction converts the ideal into the ordeal, into a torture which is now affirmed for its own sake, fueled by the martyr's fervor. The tortures of hell become the *norm* of poetic determination: since *to determine* is *to be determined*, one is determined to endure the contradiction, to obey damnation as predestination. But if the determinations of hell are an adequate figure for the intractable problem of *orientation toward* the void, they are not an adequate figure for the absolute emptiness of the void itself. In fact, obedience to the destiny of failure in seeking "the void, and the black, and the bare" will amount to surrendering the pursuit of *the void* in recognition of *the actual*. As we will see in the following chapter, the attainment of this social recognition is just as central to the achievement of *Les Fleurs du Mal* as its treatment of Luciferian logic.

The point of the analysis above is not simply to rehearse the racializing parameters of angel/whore tropes in Baudelaire's poetry, but to situate those parameters with conceptual precision vis-à-vis the problem of poetic determination. To review: the poetic problem of figuring the absolute is minimally active in the determination of the blank page by material signifiers. The discordant irony introduced into the harmony of ideas by an Idea of the void drawn from the Form of emptiness falls from the Being of *le Diable* into the irony of inscription, of the *mélange* it entails. Passing through the idealized figure of the "Creole Lady," this irony finds its adequately conflictual referent in the mixed-race mistress as *mal ange*, merging once more with satanic determination. We might thus recognize that in *Les Fleurs du Mal* figurations of race and miscegenation respond, symptomatically, to a problem of determination situated at the crux of idea, figure, and sign—of metaphysics, theology, and the materiality of writing—rendering this also a *historical* problem infiltrated by the modern history of colonialism and slavery. Offering a solution to one problem (how to figure the irony of signifying the void), these figurative strategies give way onto others Baudelaire is less inclined to work through. There is a historical-metaphysical-semiotic complex at work in the figures of the creole and the tenebrous mistress that the poems cannot process, though they index permutations of its partially sublated pressure.

Baudelaire is not oblivious to what goes unsaid in those poems where we find race at the intersection of sex and history. In an essay on Poe, Baudelaire lists with bitter sarcasm "a few outstanding traits, a few examples of morality from the noble country of Franklin," and he begins with "burning chained-up negroes, guilty of having felt their black cheeks tingle with the flush of honour."[62] Slavery is not a mere idyll in Baudelaire's psyche, but that does not prevent him from representing it as such, and the scorn he dispenses toward the "biblical hypocrisy" of American morality is not meted out with equal stringency to French colonialism. Slavery and colonialism can be alluded to, but it seems the historical realities those allusions occlude could not enter the poems without running the risk of the "crowning modern heresy—didacticism."[63] Baudelaire *does* find a symbol, an image, an allegory for the brutal violence of modern colonialism in "Voyage to Cythera," which we will examine in the following chapter. But because that will be an image he can identify with, it avoids or displaces the relation between

62 Chareles Baudelaire, "Further Notes on Edgar Poe" in *Selected Writings on Art and Literature*, trans. P.E. Charvet (New York: Penguin, 1972), 197.
63 Baudelaire, "Further Notes on Edgar Poe," 208.

colonialism and race. The pressure of history upon the poetic figures of miscegenation will be suppressed as it is indexed because those figures are allotted the task of *mitigating* the irony of the void, rather than confronting it. That is why the failure of that mitigation breeds such anguish.

Given the pressure of what goes unsaid, of the return of the repressed, of the failed mitigation of the absolute, one might just want to forget and be forgotten.

> Et Temps m'engloutit minute par minute,
> Comme la neige immense un corps pris de roideur;
> — Je contemple d'en haut le globe en sa rondeur
> Et je n'y cherche plus l'abri d'une cahute.
>
> Avalanche, veux-tu m'emporter dans ta chute?
>
> —
>
> And Time engulfs me minute by minute,
> Like the immense snow a stiffened body;
> —I gaze from on high at the globe in its round
> And I no longer look for a sheltering hut.
>
> Avalanche, will you carry me off in your fall? [64]

If the signifier cannot evoke mediations of the void without its irony drawing more onto the page than one would like to include, and if one cannot drown the page in ink and still be a poet, would it be possible to be buried *underneath* the page? Apparently above it all, gazing on high at the globe in its round, the altitude of the speaker does not suffice to evade the passage of Time, akin to an avalanche from which one no longer seeks shelter. *Wanting* to forget entails a will to forget what will *become* of history, "minute by minute." To the question—What may I hope for?—the regulative harmony of ideas answers: the

[64] FE, 264-265.

progressive unification of our knowledge, the development of social institutions in accordance with the moral law, and the rewards of a future life in proportion to our worthiness to be happy. But the discord of that regulative harmony, not least the historical manifestations of that discord and their unconscious symptoms, are exhausting:

> Morne esprit, autrefois amoureux de la lutte,
> L'Espoir, dont l'éperon attisait ton ardeur,
> Ne veut plus t'enfourcher! Couche-toi sans pudeur,
> Vieux cheval dont le pied à chaque obstacle butte.
>
> Résigne-toi, mon coeur; dors ton sommeil de brute.

—

> Dreary spirit, once enamored of struggle,
> Hope, whose spur pricked your ardor,
> No longer wants to mount you! Sleep shamelessly,
> Old horse whose hoof strikes every obstacle.
>
> Resign yourself, my heart; sleep your bestial sleep.

Baudelaire's "intoxication in 1848," retrospectively annotated as "Taste for vengeance. *Natural* pleasure of demolition,"[65] gives way to a "Taste for Nothingness" that would defer even the responsibility for self-erasure to natural disaster. If politics is the struggle to engage historical contradiction—a confrontation with figural reveries that always produces new ones—then forgetting, in *Les Fleurs du Mal*, is a matter of forgetting politics. What remains of incessant collisions with the implacable obstacles of history is resignation, and it remains only to be swept away.

Against all odds, but also inevitably, we find a figure of such resigned forgetting that manages to fuse the immense snow of

---

65 Baudelaire, *Oeuvres Complètes* I, 679.

Time (the inescapable avalanche) with the warm haze of Africa (the desert of elsewhere), the oblivion of the blank white page with the persistent obduracy of the signifier: a figure of the void not as that to which one aspires toward but rather as that which is forgotten.

> Rien n'égale en longueur les boiteuses journées,
> Quand sous les lourds flocons des neigeuses années
> L'ennui, fruit de la morne incuriosité,
> Prend les proportions de l'immortalité.
> — Désormais tu n'es plus, ô matière vivante!
> Qu'un granit entouré d'une vague épouvante,
> Assoupi dans le fond d'un Sahara brumeux;
> Un vieux sphinx ignoré du monde insoucieux,
> Oublié sur la carte, et dont l'humeur farouche
> Ne chante qu'aux rayons du soleil qui se couche.
>
> —
>
> Nothing equals in length of limping days,
> When beneath heavy flakes of snowy years
> Ennui, fruit of bleak incuriosity,
> Takes on the proportions of immortality.
> —Then you are no more, o living matter!
> Than a stone attended by a vague terror,
> Sunk in the depths of a hazy Sahara;
> An old sphinx ignored by insouciant society,
> Overlooked on the map, and whose fierce humor
> Sings only to rays of the setting sun.[66]

Just as the charms of the Creole Lady are "ignoré," the old sphinx is "oublié." Like her, he will only be introduced to the "vrai pays de gloire" through the poem in which he appears: the sphinx is forgotten or overlooked on the map by "insouciant society," but Baudelaire's metaphor is not overlooked in anthologies of

---

66 FE, 256-257.

French literature. Ennui does indeed take on the proportions of immortality through the inscription of living matter in inorganic signifiers "attended by a vague terror," like the reading of a tale by Poe. The power of this poem lies in the contradiction between its content and its reception. This contradiction blazes with dialectical force and fierce humor as the words "nothing," "no more," and "ignored" are minutely qualified by "only" in the final line, which offers a sole exception to perennial oblivion. The old sphinx sings only to the rays of the setting sun, which cannot hear its song, but it is light that illuminates the signs we see. The implacable irony of figurative failure wells up as the curiously redemptive mirage of reading; the poem cannot eliminate the silence of its apparition, and though it appears in the visual field only as a series of unexceptional marks, it is absolutely beautiful. Its figure of the forgotten is remembered for that reason. The beauty of the poem is bound to a certain ideological desperation: *there must be* a desert of snow wherein the determinations of Ennui, of one's own failures and misprisions, of the obstacles of history, of the hypocrisy of Europe, of "progress," of the derelictions of Time can sing from the depths in which they are buried, from the depths of a miscreant century. But the desperation of that beauty does not annul it, which is why it somehow registers an unconscious and a painful hope, one in conflict with itself and bound to a discordant ideal, a hope lodged *in* the unconscious, in the deserted memory of the forgotten, the hope *of* the unconscious, which we cannot help but feel even if we reject it—an irremediable beauty.

It is an *apocalyptic* hope, given only to the revelations of reading, through which the image is revealed as unseen. It is no coincidence that in those poems devoted to the representation of apocalypse—the triumph of Void over Soul, World, and God—Baudelaire will proceed by way of ekphrasis. Poetic determination will operate at one remove, taking as its object a representation that has *already* figured the void, such that these figurations can be subtracted from the visual field and offered to imaginative construction from the bare bones of the letter. In "A Fantastic Engraving," Baudelaire's ekphrastic representation of Mortimer's *Death on a Pale Horse* [Figure 4] begins in a relatively straightforward descriptive register:

> Ce spectre singulier n'a pour toute toilette,
> Grotesquement campé sur son front de squelette,
> Qu'un diadème affreux sentant le carnaval.
> Sans éperons, sans fouet, il essouffle un cheval,
> Fantôme comme lui, rosse apocalyptique,
> Qui bave des naseaux comme un épileptique.
>
> —
>
> This singular specter has nothing to wear but,
> Grotesquely set on his skeletal brow,
> A ghastly diadem reeking of carnival.
> Without spurs, without whip, he wearies his horse,
> A phantom like him, apocalyptic nag,
> Whose nostrils foam like an epileptic.[67]

Here the poem determines our relation to elements of the image through interpretive description. What we are looking at is a *specter*; the diadem is *ghastly* and its appearance on the brow is *grotesque*; the horse is a *phantom* but also *like an epileptic*—immaterial and yet intensely corporeal. But negative description is even more central to work of ekphrasis, since it allows the poem to present what we *do not* see in the visual work: the specter has *nothing* to wear but his crown[68] (in the image he is partially covered by drapery); he is *without* spurs and *without* whip. Objects are offered to imagination as absent, such that what *would not*

---

67 FE, 246-247.
68 Baudelaire brilliantly exploits the grammatical suspension of ne...que across the opening three lines of the poem. My translation tries to retain the structure of the qualified negation, though Baudelaire does not refer directly to *rien*.

FIGURE 4: John Hamilton Mortimer, *Death on a Pale Horse*, ca. 1775

be seen takes its place alongside what *would* be seen, were we looking at the engraving rather than reading a poem. This negative background foregrounds the fact that what we imagine is not what we see—that what is given to sensation (signifiers) is not the referent called forth in intuition (this singular specter), since the latter must be produced by imagination in the absence of an object.

Ekphrasis involves a double negation of the relay between sensation and intuition, and the effect of this double negation is to draw near the purely *formal* ground of intuition itself. First negation: a poem is ekphrastic insofar as it describes a visual artwork, but it is not exactly a *representation* of the artwork that we are given through description. The poem breaks the relay between sensation and intuition, since it is now the description *itself* that is the basis of an intuition without the presence of an object. Second negation: but *there is* an object of intuition given through sensation—the materiality of the signifier. Yet this object, this series of objects (the poem), is also not what we are to hold in our mind's eye. The materiality of the poem negates that of the image, but the imagined image negates the materiality of the poem. What would be the incoherence of this double negation is mitigated by the fact that "the image" does not have the same sense in each case. On the one hand, the materiality of writing negates the receptivity of intuition (the perception of the artwork described). On the other hand, the appearance of the materiality of writing *through* the receptivity of intuition is negated by the productivity of imagination which the signifier stimulates. One sense of the image is material (e.g. an engraving); the other sense of the image is immaterial (a phantasy). At the crux of these two aspects of the image—these two different relationships of "image" to intuition—is the mere form of intuition itself. It is the *formal emptiness* of intuition that enables its receptivity to accommodate either *sensations* (material) or *objects of imagination* (immaterial). Neither "the poem" nor "the artwork" it describes are adequate to the productivity of imagination generated by their relation and by their mutual negations. The negativity of this "neither" is made possible by *nothing*: the mere form of intuition, without substance. Ekphrasis thus involves a paradoxical effort to isolate the mere form of intuition by negating the visual image while still populating intuition with unpresented objects. It attempts to isolate intuition from sensation while still prompting the imagination, through those minimal sensations that signifiers are, to produce intuitions that are not objects of experience. Through the empirical (reading) we access the *a priori*: this singular specter has nothing to wear. The ekphrasis of apocalypse has a particularly intimate relationship to the essence of this rhetorical form: apocalypse is the thematic semblable of the formal fact that ekphrasis always orients us toward the void by drawing us into knowledge of nothing.

The next two lines of the poem—its central sentence—distill this essence of ekphrasis, exploding the representational relation between poem and engraving (seen/unseen) by formulating metaphysical implications of its allegory that can only be *thought*:

> Au travers de l'espace ils s'enfoncent tous deux,
> Et foulent l'infini d'un sabot hasardeux.
>
> —
>
> The two of them sink as they pass through space,
> And trample the infinite with hazardous hoof.

What is at issue across these two lines is the relation between pure intuition and pure reason, between *concept* of nothing and *idea* of the void. Specter and phantom pass through space, but this is neither the visual space of the engraving, nor the space in which the material sensation of the poem is given. They pass through the empty space of pure intuition, in which we try (impossibly?) to imagine figures sinking into emptiness. As they pass they "trample the infinite": the idea itself falls underfoot, like the dead tread down by Beauty and crushed by the implacable daylight specter in "The Seven Old Men." It is as though figural presentation of the mere form of intuition, objects sinking into emptiness without object, tramples the very contradiction the image entails, destroys the absolute void toward which it tends. The contradiction is condensed in the evocation of an impossible object—a hazardous hoof—a *nihil negativum*, the empty object without a concept, like a two-sided rectilinear figure. The hazardous hoof is a figure of *contingency as object*, and thus a conceptless object, since pure contingency cannot be *understood* as a determinate being. The figure welds necessity and contingency (figuring the arbitrary nature of fate), since the logical incoherence of the figure is necessary to its identity. Straining toward the idea of the void, the imagination falls back into the division of the concept of nothing, circling clockwise: #3 empty intuition without an object (space), #4 empty object without a concept (hazardous hoof), #2 empty object of a concept (specter), #1 empty concept without object (apocalypse). Apocalypse is the noumenal residue of annihilation, the revelation of what lies behind the veil of experience, the midnight noon of nothing.

In the element of the unthinkable, where the concept touches the disharmony of ideas, the undead cavalier tramples not only the infinite but also the "nameless hordes." In Mortimer's engraving, his empty eyes peer out across the picture plane at an indeterminate tangent to the viewer's gaze, as the skeleton

> ...parcourt, comme un prince inspectant sa maison,
> Le cimetière immense et froid, sans horizon,
> Où gisent, aux lueurs d'un soleil blanc et terne,
> Les peuples de l'histoire ancienne et moderne.
>
> —
>
> ...surveys, like a prince inspecting his home,
> The horizonless cemetery, cold and immense,
> Where lie, amid dull and white glimmers of sun,
> The people of ancient and modern history.

Where knowledge of nothing brushes up against the idea of the void, even the distinction between the ancient and the modern is laid to rest. The space of that unthinkable encounter is a "horizonless cemetery" where the boundary between the living and the dead is undone. Again, this limitless undoing depends upon the gap opened by ekphasis between poem and engraving: neither the borders of the picture nor the formal finitude of the poem contain the absence of the image. It dwells in imagination, but the substance of what we are called to imagine is emptiness without substance: the burial of the infinite in cold immensity.

It is in the late ekphrastic masterpiece, "Danse Macabre," that the impasses and contradictions of figuring the void achieve a dark humor adequate to their absurdity. With that strange unity of concision and superfluity so characteristic of Baudelaire's style, the first quatrain distills the tone of Ernest Christophe's pithy statuette [Figure 5]:

> Fière, autant qu'un vivant, de sa noble stature,
> Avec son gros bouquet, son mouchoir et ses gants,
> Elle a la nonchalance et la désinvolture
> D'une coquette maigre aux airs extravagants.
>
> —
>
> Proud, as any among the living, of noble stature,
> With her great bouquet, her handkerchief and gloves,
> She has the nonchalance and flippancy
> Of a skinny coquette with extravagant airs.[69]

If the void had a style, would it not unite the concise and superfluous, at once "maigre" and "extravagant"? As the poem will tell us, Christophe's figure answers to Baudelaire's most cherished inclination ("Tu répond, grand squelette, à mon goût le plus cher!"); it not only accords with his taste but also expresses the peculiar savor of his poetry. And it only takes one syllable, held

---

69 FE, 326-331.

FIGURE 5: Ernest Christophe, Untitled Statuette, ca. 1858

aloft by a haughty caesura, "Fière," to communicate the upright bearing of statuary in the medium of poetic rhythm. This is not a stiff, but a nonchalant and easy pride. Like the rhyme of "farouche" with "se couche" in "Spleen," the combination of "Fière" and "désinvolture" shares the mood of the cats that slink through *Les Fleurs du Mal*, which shadow the quality of Baudelaire's imagination. Here this feline tonality of the soul is fused with the soulless nonchalance of a *squelette* of the demi-monde.

Our attention is drawn to the negative composition of her eyes:

Ses yeux profonds sont faits de vide et de ténèbres,
Et son crâne, des fleurs artistement coiffé,
Oscille mollement sur ses frêles vertèbres.
Ô charme d'un néant follement attifé!

—

Her deep eyes are made of void and of shadow,
And her skull, with flowers artistically coiffed,
Wobbles gently upon her frail vertebrae.
O the charm of a nothingness dressed to the nines!

Rhyming "ténèbres" with "vertèbres" formalizes the embodiment of the void expressed by eyes opening onto the darkness of a hollow skull. The proud bearing of the skull is supported by a frail column, and the frailty of pride provokes a celebration of artifice, the charm of nothing's extravagant attire. "Fashion must therefore be thought of as a symptom of the taste for the ideal that floats on the surface in the human brain, above all the coarse, earthly and disgusting things that life according to nature accumulates, as a sublime distortion of nature."[70] But a symptom of the taste for *what* ideal? The "distortion" ("déformation") of nature indexed by fashion is the symptom of a discordant

---

70 Baudelaire, "The Painter of Modern Life" in *Selected Writings on Art and Literature*, 426.

ideal that draws the dialectic of its irony continually back into itself. Thus it floats as an immaterial *effect*, never stabilizing into substance, never resolving into unity, drawing us ever beyond experience yet never quite into the absolute, a divided ideal which is not that of the highest good but rather one involving the complications of conscience, the misdirections of desire, the perversions of reason: an ideal including artifice as an aspect of truth.

The first of many rhetorical questions we encounter in the poem captures the social psyche of this ideal deformation of nature in a sidelong query, perhaps issued *sotta voce* by a fascinated suitor or gnashed in silence by a jealous rival: "Was there ever so narrow a waist at the ball?" ("Vit-on jamais au bal une taille plus mince?"). The line slyly conveys the *nihilism* implicit in social determinations of femininity, of "woman," also whispered in "Confession":

« Que c'est un dur métier que d'être belle femme,
    Et que c'est le travail banal
De la danseuse folle et froide que se pâme
    Dans son sourire machinel;

« Que bâtir sur les coeurs est une chose sotte;
    Que tout craque, amour et beauté,
Jusqu'à ce que l'Oubli les jette dans sa hotte
    Pour les rendre à l'Éternité. »

—

"What hard work to be a beautiful woman,
    And how banal the labor
Of the cold and demented dancer who swoons
    In her machinic smile;

"How stupid it is to take things to heart;
    How things fall apart, love and beauty,

> Until Oblivion throws them into its sack
> And turns them over to Eternity."[71]

That the ideal waist would be as narrow as a spinal column is not only the *reductio ad absurdum* of gender, of the hard work of being a beautiful woman, it also ironizes the founding of *all* regulative norms upon absolutes, however disavowed. Christophe's *squelette* is the figure of absolute woman, and Woman does not exist. But the tone here is predominately comic. The line *plays* with the absurdity of gender, it manifests an enjoyment of its strange games and its lovely masquerades:

> Sa robe exagérée, en sa royale ampleur,
> S'écroule abondamment sur un pied sec que pince
> Un soulier pomponné, joli comme une fleur.
>
> —
>
> Her exorbitant gown, in its regal plenitude,
> Drapes abundantly over a dry foot pinched
> In a pompomed slipper, pretty as a flower.

To defamiliarize the relation of beauty to the artifice of fashion *and* the prettiness of a rose (the regal plenitude of a gown above a dry pinched foot), one need only subtract the flesh and decorate "the nameless elegance of human armature." *Pomponné* denatures the flower as it decorates the slipper, and it condenses all the ceremony of social presentation into a word with the offhanded self-evidence of *dada*, the kind self-evidence that amounts to its own justification—all the abundance of nature and culture in a dryly admiring synecdoche. Poetry.

Again the double negation of ekphrasis is mobilized to elaborate phenomenal predicates and suggest social worlds while drawing them toward the formal emptiness of the metaphysical *a priori* which is their condition of possibility:

---

[71] FE, 172-175.

Le gouffre de tes yeux, plein d'horribles pensées,
Exhale le vertige, et les danseurs prudents
Ne contempleront pas sans d'amères nausées
Le sourire éternel de tes trente-deux dents.

—

The abyss of your eyes, full of horrible thoughts,
Exhales vertigo, and the prudent dancers
Cannot behold without bitter nausea
The eternal smile of your thirty-two teeth.

Ekphrasis imparts horrible thoughts to unthinking matter, breathes vertigo into solid substance, conjures prudent dancers at an invisible ball whose nausea stems from intimations of their inexistence. "The abyss of your eyes" deploys the double address of apostrophe—to the figure *outside* the poem and the reader *of* the poem—to suggest not only the vacancy of the statuette's gaze but its absence from our own visual field, as our eyes flicker over its verbal description rather than the statuette itself. The poem then turns apostrophic address toward querying the universal:

Pourtant, qui n'a serré dans ses bras un squelette,
Et qui ne s'est nourri des choses du tombeau?

—

Yet, who has not clutched a skeleton in his arms,
And who has not fed upon things of the grave?

Note that the "I" of "Obsession"—"Car je cherche le vide, et le noir, et le nu!"—has become the we, or rather, the "who" of rhetorical universality. *There is no one*, it is implied, who has not clutched a skeleton, and who does not feed upon things of the grave. The implied answer to the rhetorical question is the same one Odysseus puts in the mouth of the Cyclops, who delivers Homer's dialectical memento mori: *no one is killing me*. You (*squelette*) becomes who (no one), and around this hinge, turned by the rhetoric of ekphrasis, by its desubstantialization of phenomenal experience, the "tu" that had been addressed to the statuette becomes a "vous" that includes the whole "mortal herd" and the "tes" of "risible Humanity" in general.

Here is the poem's raucous and careening finale, spoken by the *néant* herself:

« Ô squelettes musqués,

« Antinoüs flétris, dandys à face glabre,
Cadavres vernissés, lovelaces chenus,
Le branle universel de la danse macabre
Vous entraîne en des lieux qui ne sont pas connu!

« Des quais froids de la Seine aux bords brûlants du Gange,
Le troupeau mortel saute et se pâme, sans voir
Dans un trou du plafond la trompette de l'Ange
Sinistrement béante ainsi qu'un tromblon noir.

« En tout climat, sous tout soleil, la Mort t'admire
En tes contorsions, risible Humanité,
Et souvent, comme toi, se parfumant de myrrhe,
Mêle son ironie à ton insanité! »

—

"O musky skeletons,

"Withered Antinoi, dandies with glabrous faces,
Varnished cadavers, hoary lovelaces,
The universal jerk of the danse macabre
Sweeps you off to unknown places!

"From cold quays of the Seine to burning shores of the Ganges,
The mortal herd skips and swoons, not seeing
The Angel's horn in a hole in the ceiling
Gaping sinisterly like a black blunderbuss.

"In every clime, under every sun, Death admires
Your contortions, risible Humanity,
And often, like you, scents herself with myrrh,
Mingling her irony with your insanity!"

Antinous and the dandy, withered antiquity and glabrous modernity of the masculine ideal, will be swept alike into the unknown. Every *different* place, from the Seine to the Ganges, is determined as the same site of the unseen. "Without seeing" is a crucial trope of ekphrastic apocalypse: the horn of the allegorical Angel is outside the frame of the picture and invisible to the blind sculptural figure. By way of the signifier, we know without looking up that it protrudes through "a hole in the ceiling," that it gapes "like a black blunderbuss." It would seem impossible to imagine an *object* that could figure the eruption of the void from the nothingness of empty intuition *without an object*, but Baudelaire proves once more that he is a skilled guide to the underworld: one would have to not see the hollow bore of a gun gaping through a hole.

Lured toward the void by love of disform, ekphrasis becomes our ironic beacon. It leads us along the *via negativa* of empty intuition, turning the phenomenal determinacy of the visible into the ephemeral fluency of meaning, while drawing singular specters of imagination from the gap between these two senses of *sense*. And as we see in "Danse Macabre," *apocalyptic* ekphrasis also draws our attention to the skeleton of the signifier. We might note, for example, the mildly sinister look of a word like *désinvolture*, a word whose sense conveys the aristocratic flippancy of «Qu'ils mangent de la brioche» or "I would prefer not to"—a word that takes a nap on the scaffold, a prince born of the dead-letter office. It is not just the idea of the void, but more importantly its discordant relation to the harmony of ideas that sows disengagement amid the signs of good sense, and that drives us to look for the unseen in some unknown place, where there might be a forgotten sphinx to riddle our ignorance, our knowledge of nothing, with its unheard song.

"Mingling her irony with your insanity"—this is not only the disposition of Death, but also of Reason. Perhaps it is through the ironic twist of that *not only*, mingling Death with Reason in the element of madness, that Thought and Void become one. How exquisitely scentless, the trace of their perfume on the page.

To Look Without Loathing

Reason is akin to Death in that it is voracious. "La tombe attend; elle est avide!"[72] À *vide*: such is the destination of both infinite thought and the finite body. Confronted with any determinate particular, reason drags it toward the absolute, just as death drags corporeal determinacy toward dissolution. Thus, we have tried to show that the pursuit of the void in *Les Fleurs du Mal* is a rational pursuit, stemming from the relation of reason to the concept of nothing, which has to be thought in excess of the logical function of negation. The circuitous pathways of this pursuit—due to the discord among ideas introduced by the void and the poetic irony of approaching the void through figuration—account for many of the complexities and much of the anguish the poems include and express. There is an anguish of reason: that of a finite being in whom the faculty of infinite thought is lodged, such that the body itself may suffer the force of the disjunction. It is thus a conflict within the Ideal itself that gives rise to Spleen, that draws Spleen into the Ideal and the Ideal into Spleen—a more structurally complex and conceptually interesting dialectic than a duality of human nature, of virtue and sin, of happy poems and sad poems. It is at the level of the contradictory Ideal—not in the opposition of Ideal and Spleen—that a poem like "Danse Macabre" finds the source of its humor and profundity, both of which reside in the mingling of irony and insanity not only with each other, but also with reason.

But of course not all the pathways of *Les Fleurs du Mal* lead into the chicanes of the absolute. Though an orientation toward the void is among the metaphysical tendencies of the volume, it

---

72 FE, 206-209.

has many other projects, other sources of irony, other impasses and obsessions. If the pursuit of the unconditioned does not exhaust the vocation of the poems, though it may be exhausting, our question will be: how is it that poetry constructs modes of thinking and feeling that resist the undertow of the absolute, that remain at the level of the particular, of relations among conditions, yet without disavowing the emotional force and the rational necessity of the unconditioned?

This last clause specifies the real locus of the problem, for one can always *pretend* to secure the particular by turning away from the universal, rejecting abstraction, pointing to the given and circumscribing poiesis within the domain of whatever abstraction one chooses, ironically, as a delimitation: the historical, the local, the material, the concrete, the factual, the political. Baudelaire is attentive to irony, to its corrosive persistence. He is not one to overlook the fact that such gestures amount to disavowed decisions upon the Ideal, to an image of the true or the good or the beautiful that one either fails to recognize or fails to acknowledge as a regulative idea. Baudelaire's intellectual orientation is not rigorously philosophical, but it is conceptually exacting.

Consider the influential formula of William Carlos Williams, "no ideas but in things," distilling his effort to reground the Imagist polemic against abstraction by filtering out Pound's neo-Platonist idealizations of cultural virtù, H.D.'s neo-Hellenic mythographies, and Eliot's bookish allusions. Here is the context of its articulation:

> Before the grass is out the people are out
> and bare twigs still whip the wind—
> when there is nothing, in the pause between
> snow and grass in the parks and at the street ends
> —Say it, no ideas but in things—
> nothing but the blank faces of the houses
> and cylindrical trees

    bent, forked by preconception and accident
    split, furrowed, creased, mottled, stained
    secret—into the body of the light—

    These are the ideas, savage and tender
    somewhat of the music, et cetera
    of Paterson, that great philosopher— [73]

Say it when there is nothing, in the gap between seasons, in the pause that brings forward the blankness of facades and outlines the geometry of trees, torqued by time and weather that endows them with those wounds and accretions which are the secret of their beauty, as they extend into the body of the light. What the poem doesn't say is "winter" or "spring." It doesn't say "April." It finds the terms it needs to specify the fact and feeling of a seasonal absence in the particulars it describes. "These are the ideas, savage and tender... / Of Paterson, that great philosopher." The town is the book in which the ideas of its place-name are inscribed. Locality thinks. The poet articulates attention. And it's true: one can feel the cold in the wind that whips the twigs because it is noticed that the lashing of the twigs whips the wind—because of the thingliness of the writing, how the closing sibilance of "twigs" slides into "still" while the sense of the latter word braces the elision, how the tone of that alliteration is transformed by the ghostliness of "whip the wind," just as that phrase reverses the expected order of predication.

    The poem constructs the sense of the slogan; it is a construction, not a proposition. The sense of the slogan is not portable beyond the poem. We are told to say it, as a mantra, among the empirical particulars. But it only has force, as a mantra, amid the particularity of the poetic construction in which it appears. The branches fork "into the body of the light"—but what is a body?

---

[73] William Carlos Williams, *The Collected Poems of Williams Carlos Williams:1909-1939*, Vol. 1, Ed. A. Walton Litz and Christopher MacGowan (New York: New Directions, 1986), 263.

The poem creates a context that compellingly answers that question: its construction of the problem provides its solution. Our point is just that the slogan has no *polemical* force. Its force depends not on what it negates but on *how* its negation is manifest, and the validity of what it polemicizes against (idealism) will depend also upon the particularity of its instantiation, as the slogan implies. The irony of taking the claim as a discrete proposition—"no ideas but in things"—is that its form would then negate its content. So only the poem, not the proposition, can ground the sense of the particular, which is the point. But that can also be true of a poem that says "no things but in ideas," if it is adequately constructed. Whether a poem itself should be taken as a thing or an idea isn't obvious; the relation is reversible, and sense is dialectical.

What is at issue is the relation of "ideas," in the colloquial sense, to Ideas, in the philosophical sense, their tendential absolutism. Allegorical signifiers are the descendants of Ideas. "Paterson, that great philosopher" is made of up social particulars, people—"Inside the bus one sees / his thoughts sitting and standing"[74]—but insofar as "he" has a proper name he participates, also, in the allegory of "America," for which the enthusiasm of Williams never wanes. Williams wants to ground that allegory in particulars:

> What pathos, what mercy
> of nurses (who keep birthday books)
> and doctors who can't speak proper english— [75]

But the particularity of the poems does not suffice to prevent ideas that are not things from leading him, like anyone else, toward ideological hyperbole: "Of mixed ancestry, I felt from earliest childhood that America was the only home I could ever possibly call my own. I felt that it was expressly founded for

---

74 Williams, *Collected Poems*, 264.
75 Williams, *Collected Poems*, 265.

me, personally, and that it must be my first business in life to possess it."⁷⁶ Allegorical signifiers ("America") register the material effects of ideas that are not things. When Baudelaire propagates a slogan—"To the bottom of the Unknown to discover the *new*!"⁷⁷—he marks the unthingliness of ideas, their orientation toward an absolute (the Void), by conferring a majuscule, while no doubt grasping the irony of doing so through the thingliness of the letter. Since beauty is not only a word but its referent, and since that referent is not a thing, it is written: Beauty. Baudelaire's commitment to allegorical style is not a commitment to "idealism" but to this kind of honesty and this kind of irony.

The point is not a dispute between materialism and idealism as it bears upon poetics. The point is rather that it is only under the condition of poetic determination, displacing the opposition of materialism and idealism, that Baudelaire's famous lines may be invested with the dialectical pathos of a historically situated psychological event:

> Paris change! mais rien dans ma mélancolie
> N'a bougé! palais neufs, échafaudages, blocs,
> Vieux faubourgs, tout pour moi devient allégorie,
> Et mes chers souvenirs sont plus lourds que des rocs.
>
> —
>
> Paris changes! but nothing in my melancholy
> Has stirred! new palaces, scaffoldings, blocks,
> Old suburbs, for me everything becomes allegory,
> And my cherished memories more weighty than rocks.⁷⁸

---

76 William Carlos Williams, Letter to Horace Gregory, July 22, 1939 in *Selected Letters of Williams Carlos Williams*, ed. John C. Thirlwall (New York: New Directions, 1985), 179.

77 FE, 455.

78 FE, 292-297.

Melancholy is a psychological constant amid materially inscribed historical changes, and it seems to be the tension between stasis of mood and alteration of city that breeds the *becoming* of allegory from material particulars, and the transformation of memory into obdurate matter. For the heft of that transmutation to matter, for it to signify a *particular* transformation, there has to have been and to be a sense in which ideas may be elsewhere than in things, such that they may *now* take on the solidity of objects. How to sustain oneself within the particular without denying the pull of the rational beyond the empirical? How to mediate the rational and the empirical, without denying the persistent force the absolute, its ineradicable relevance?

* * *

At first, there's just the shadow of a doubt: "Car je cherche le vide, et le noir, et le nu! / Mais les ténèbres sont elles-mêmes des toiles."[79] We cannot yet take up the question of what "toiles" means here, though we will give it our full attention in the following chapter. For now, we only need to focus on the beginning of that second line: "Mais les ténèbres...." Even here the sense is complex, at once phenomenal, epistemological, affective, religious: a shadowy darkness, the obscurity of doubt, a sense of spiritual crisis or uncertainty, the Catholic ceremonies whose central element is the gradual extinction of candles. Perhaps most importantly, "Ténèbres" is the title of Gautier's great poem, singled out by Baudelaire as a "prodigious symphony" comparable to Beethoven, deriving from an intensity of melancholy amounting to "catholic terror."[80] Gautier's poem is apocalyptic, moving from evocations of unmourned death, through the tragically arbitrary distinction between the blessed and the cursed, to the annihilation of a world unredeemed by a second coming:

79 FE, 262-263.
80 Baudelaire, "Théophile Gautier" in *Selected Writings on Art and Literature*, 281.

Le soleil désolé, penchant son œil de feu,
Pleure sur l'univers une larme sanglante;
L'ange dit à la terre un éternel adieu.

—

The desolate sun, bending its fiery eye,
Sheds upon the universe a bloody tear;
The angel bids the earth an eternal adieu.[81]

Gautier's poem belongs to a despairing orientation toward the void. In "Obsession," on the other hand, reference to "les ténèbres" seems to qualify that orientation. Immediately following the most direct assertion of devotion to absolute emptiness in *Les Fleurs du Mal* (in a poem written in 1860, composed in a position to reflect upon the whole) we find the volume's most direct concession to mediation. The *mais* with which the final quatrain begins indicates a difference between "the void, and the black, and the bare" and dark*ness*, perhaps a quality of the dark that is not absolute but rather relational, shadowy—the darkness of a church after the extinguishing of candles, but not the total emptiness of a sky without stars.

It is as if there remains just this grammatical qualification opening the closing tercet of the sonnet —"Mais les ténèbres"— to register the *determinate* absence of the wished away stars, the trace of the extinguished, the residue of their having been that would still qualify the darkness and draw the pursuit of the absolute void into the uncertainty of the shadows. The qualification seems to concede that while the stars are wished away, they actually remain: the absolute night of their absence *would* please the speaker, *but* they are still there. The qualification marks the remainder of an unfulfilled wish, rather than of what is wished away. It is through this difference between idea and phenomenon, between the void and the darkness, absolute emptiness

---

81 Théophile Gautier, "Ténèbres" (1837) in *Oeuvres Poétique Complètes*, ed. Michel Brix (Paris: Bartillat, 2004), 189. My translation.

and relational shadow, desire and facticity, that we can begin to construct the poetic world wherein *the actual* will attain a ground in *Les Fleurs du Mal*, and through which the social will attain a fragile, dubious, and painfully generous cohesion—a tenebrous cohesion. Moreover, we will see that it is only at the level of *the book* that such a world can be constructed, only through the relational texture of the poems that the gradually fabricated ground of the actual, of the conditioned, can be articulated and sustained without disavowing desire for the unconditioned.

The qualification of the void by darkness and shadow is the phenomenal index of some minimal persistence of light, or even a conceptual trace of the relational opposition between darkness and light. This relational trace, minimal appearance or logical intimation of light, is denoted throughout *Les Fleurs du Mal* by one of the volume's most importance signifiers: *lueur*, or glimmer. Cast upon the emptiness of the void, the signs of ineliminable determination are glimmers within shadowy worlds. In "Evening Twilight" the demons bump into shutters as they traverse the glimmers tormented by the wind ("À travers les lueurs que tourment le vent").[82] In "Gambling" enormous lamps project their glimmers upon the tenebrous brows of illustrious poets ("Et d'énormes quinquets projetant leurs lueurs / Sur des fronts ténébreux de poètes illustres").[83] In "Damned Women," women within the silent hollow of pagan caves call upon Bacchus to assuage their fevers by the glimmer of crumbling resin ("aux lueurs des résines croulantes").[84] In "A Fantastic Engraving" it is the glimmers of a dull and white sun that minimally illuminate the apocalyptic expanse of the horizonless cemetery ("aux lueurs d'un soleil blanc et terne").[85] And in "Sympathetic Horror" it is in the glimmer of torn skies that the speaker locates a *reflection* of damned contentment:

82 FE, 320-323.
83 FE, 324-325.
84 FE, 390-393.
85 FE, 246-247.

> Cieux déchirés comme des grèves,
> En vous se mire mon orgueil;
> Vos vastes nuages en deuil
>
> Sont les corbillards de mes rêves,
> Et vos lueurs sont le reflet
> De l'Enfer où mon coeur se plaît.
>
> —
>
> Skies torn like shores,
> In you my pride is mirrored;
> Your vast clouds in mourning
>
> Are the hearses of my dreams,
> And your glimmers the reflection
> Of Hell where my heart is happy.[86]

If the lyric speaker of "Obsession" dreams of "the void, and the black, and the bare" through the figure of an empty black sky, then clouds will figure the hearses of his dreams, while torn skies will mirror the rending of his pride by the unattainability of the absolute. A heart that *would* be pleased by the void of a starless sky will have to settle for contentment in figural failure, "the Hell where my heart is happy," and it is thus the contentment of damnation, its sense of resolution, that is reflected in the glimmers of a riven sky. The minimal illumination of the glimmer is doubled by the mediation of reflection, which mirrors the diremption of damnation, such that mourning the loss of the absolute itself becomes a residual pleasure, a melancholic compensation for the tear between "Car je cherche..." and "Mais...."

Perhaps most importantly, we find the term *lueur* among the fragile singularities listed in the closing lines of "Hymn to Beauty":

---

86 FE, 268-269.

> De Satan ou de Dieu, qu'importe? Ange ou Sirène,
> Qu'importe, si tu rends, — fée aux yeux de velours,
> Rhythme, parfum, lueur, ô mon unique reine! —
> L'univers moins hideux et les instants moins lourds?
>
> —
>
> From Satan from of God, who cares? Angel or Siren,
> Who cares, if you render, —velvet-eyed fairy,
> Rhythm, fragrance, glimmer, o my unique queen! —
> The universe less hideous and the instants less heavy?[87]

Here the singularity of Beauty renders teleology irrelevant. It interrupts totality by lightening the instant. Beauty is the triumph of the unique over the absolute and thus of imagination over reason. That is: the aesthetic experience of the beautiful requires the particularity of temporal, spatial, sensory synthesis—though it consists in the reflective appreciation of the *feeling* of that synthesis, rather than in the determining cognition of the *objectivity* of the given. It is thus the triumph of imagination over understanding as well. The "velvet-eyed fairy" is the figure of Baudelaire's Queen of the Faculties, which evades the moral determinacy of Angel or Siren without thereby falling into pure indetermination. Beauty has a texture: it is not any particular color—blue, green, brown, or grey—but velvet-eyed, the richly delicate feeling of whatever shades may glimmer therein, less the meaning than the sound of "moins hideux," less the carelessness than the precise insouciance of "qu'importe," that commitment to the noncommittal that lends "aestheticism" its dialectical depth and its singular morality. This accounts for the imperious aspect, the inhuman grandeur of Beauty, who counts Horror among her jewels and Murder among her trinkets. A lifetime of subservient devotion to capricious whims, indifferent to public mores, becomes legible as a meticulous form of respect through the delicate traceries of sounds and rhythms: "fée aux yeux de velours."

[87] FE, 100-103.

The flickering qualities of "rhythme, parfum, lueur" constitute an evanescent aesthetic medium distinguished from understanding ("un langage connu") and from reason ("le vide, et le noir, et le nu"), a medium born of the minimal difference of *les ténèbres* from both the absolute emptiness of the void and the determinacy of the constellation. We must be precise in our use of the term "aesthetic": we refer neither to immediacy of sensation (a scent), nor the determinacy of that sensation as an object of representation (the scent of perfume), nor to art or literature as the objective medium of sensation or representation. We refer to the subjective *feeling* deriving from sensation, representation, or artistic construction; and we refer to a form of feeling detached from both practical ends and sensory appetites—a feeling of form that pleases for its own sake and within which, therefore, one only wants to dwell. We refer here also to a particular type of the aesthetic: not the sublime but the beautiful, since the sublime emerges from the capture of the sensible by reason, drawing us into pursuit of the infinite, the absolute, the totality. The world that emerges from "rhythme, parfum, lueur," on the other hand, is the world of singular qualities that do not press the faculties toward the limit of conditions; rather one seeks only to linger within this world as its own reward, within the sufficiency of its affective advent.

Beauty "answers to nothing" in *Les Fleurs du Mal*. It is the figure of *disinterested* satisfaction, yet it achieves this disinterest through the *propagation* of both good and evil. It "pours confusedly beneficence and crime;" its kisses "are a philter" that "makes the hero cowardly and the child courageous." It is not only that Beauty may be *encountered* in representations of cowardice or courage, beneficence or crime; the implication is also that it *gives rise* to apparently opposing dispositions and states of affairs: it "sows at hazard joys and disasters." The aesthetic experience of beauty may be theorized, but it is constitutive of that experience, and thus of Beauty itself, that it cannot not be *understood* in its advent. "I reign in azure like an inscrutable sphinx," Beauty tells us in the sonnet bearing her name:

Je suis belle, ô mortels! comme un rêve de pierre,
Et mon sein, où chacun s'est meurtri tour à tour,
Est fait pour inspirer au poète un amour
Eternel et muet ainsi que la matière.

Je trône dans l'azur comme un sphinx incompris;
J'unis un coeur de neige à la blancheur des cygnes;
Je hais le mouvement qui déplace les lignes,
Et jamais je ne pleure et jamais je ne ris.

Les poètes, devant mes grandes attitudes,
Que j'ai l'air d'emprunter aux plus fiers monuments,
Consumeront leurs jours en d'austères études;

Car j'ai, pour fasciner ces dociles amants,
De purs miroirs que font toutes chose plus belles:
Mes yeux, mes larges yeux aux clartés éternelles!

—

I am lovely, o mortals! like a dream of stone,
And my breast, where each is bruised in turn,
Is made to inspire in the poet a love
Eternal and mute as is matter.

I reign in azure like an inscrutable sphinx;
I unite heart of snow with whiteness of swans;
I hate the movement that unsettles the lines,
And I never laugh and I never cry.

The poets, before my lofty bearing,
Of an air transposed from proudest monuments,
Consume their days in austere study;

> For I have, to fascinate these docile paramours,
> Pure mirrors that make all things more lovely:
> My eyes, my eternally lucid wide eyes![88]

The loveliness of Beauty is like a dream of stone. As a *feeling of life*, the pleasure of beauty returns us to the uncanny advent of manifestation itself, of sensing and feeling, from inorganic matter. It is an inversion of the death drive, returning us to the communion of life and matter yet tending toward the former as the unconscious wish of the latter. Beauty never laughs and it never cries because it inheres in the *form* of comedy and tragedy. It may be attended by emotion, but it is the formal substrate of the emotion it inspires. Insofar as it is merely formal, it hates the movement that unsettles the lines. This is the import of Baudelaire's Parnassian classicism: Beauty is possessed of a lofty bearing and its production requires austere study. The poet who loves it is represented in Courbet's portrait: fixated on his book, detached from all else.

Yet the love of Beauty is not only obsessive and willful; it is also a docile fascination. One is consumed *by it* and cannot quite approach it; its breast bruises those who get too close. The love it inspires depends upon life, upon feeling, but it is "Eternal and mute as is matter." Insofar as the experience of Beauty is that of *life itself* it does not accord with the *interests* of life. It is immanent to its own advent and thus has no end other than itself. It is like a dream of stone because it shears feeling away from the appetites of sensation. It is improper to cycles of reproduction, since it subtends and traverses them as the phantasm of their mute source (a dream of stone). Finally, the eyes of Beauty are "pure mirrors": beauty is reflective, and its reflective character is lucid. It is not pathologically conditioned sensation but a clarion feeling of form that dwells in the element of the universal: not everything is beautiful, but all things reflected by the mirror of the beautiful are made more lovely. Thus, Horror is not the least charming of its jewels.

---

88 FE, 90-91.

Baudelaire constructs the disinterestedness of Beauty through the reversibility of paradox, the mutual negation of normative determinations. Its minimal elements—rhythm, fragrance, glimmer—give rise to forms of subjective feeling whose satisfactions are ends in themselves and whose effects are indeterminate. If the aesthetic, according to the philosophical system that first secured its singularity, is ultimately an intimation of teleological harmony, we have already seen that *Les Fleurs du Mal* cannot evade the rationality of thinking a discord of ideas, and thus the ruin of teleology. If Beauty is a figure of the Ideal, that is not because it is an ideal harmony but because it is sufficiently inhuman, sufficiently disinterested, to survive the disharmony of the ideas, the discord of the Ideal. If the beautiful is disinterested human satisfaction, Baudelaire's allegorical figure raises Beauty to the level of disinterest in human satisfaction itself. Allegory objectifies the subjective as a subject in its own right, an objective subject. It is the subjective universality of the beautiful that justifies this poetic transformation. And that allegorical transformation merely confirms, merely thinks through, what is always implicit in reflexive objections to the distinction of the beautiful from both the agreeable and the good: beauty is frightening.

In *Les Fleurs du Mal*, however, it is insofar as beauty gives way to interest that it gives rise to ruin. In order to understand how ruin itself becomes the sole principle of family the poems will affirm, and how the community of ruins will come to invest the aesthetic with the normative, with care for the particularity of the actual, for the content of form, we must now follow the *lure* of beauty through the complex of seduction toward the agony of embodiment, and from there to the reality of the social.

Emerging from the difference between void and shadow, qualitative singularities will *mingle* in the element of the sensible. In the armoire of an abandoned house we find a flask where

Mille pensers dormaient, chrysalides funèbres,
Frémissant doucement dans les lourdes ténèbres,
Qui dégagent leur aile et prennent leur essor,
Teintés d'azur, glacés de rose, lamés d'or.

—

A thousand thoughts were sleeping, funereal chrysalides,
Rustling softly in heavy shadows,
That spread their wings and take flight,
Tints of azure, leaves of gold, glazes of rose.[89]

From the rustles of heavy shadows, chrysalides of thought take flight as would glinting butterflies, the fragile metallic tones in their wings blending across clauses. The beautiful eyes of a cat are "alloyed of metal and agate" ("Mêlés de métal et d'agate"),[90] the smoke of the author's pipe entwines and cradles his soul "in a blue and mobile mesh" ("Dans le réseau mobile et bleu"),[91] and he dreams of a room with

> Les plus rares fleurs
> Mêlant leurs odeurs
> Aux vagues senteurs de l'ambre,
>
> —
>
> The rarest flowers
> Mingling their scents
> With the faint fragrance of amber,[92]

This merging and blending of qualities and sensations is the medium of metempsychosis, of transport to "La Vie Antérieure," where

---

89 FE, 180-183.
90 FE, 140-141.
91 FE, 240-241.
92 FE, 196-199.

> Les houles, en roulant les images des cieux,
> Mêlaient d'une façon solennel et mystique
> Les tout-puissant accords de leur riche musique
> Aux couleurs de couchant reflété par mes yeux.
>
> —
>
> The swells, enfolding images of skies
> Mingled in a manner mystical and solemn
> The omnipotent accords of their rich music
> With the sunset colors reflected by my eyes.[93]

Synaesthesia draws the folding of skies within swells into the reflection of sunset in the eyes of the speaker, such that the rich music of the waves is mingled with images. Since the enfolding of sky by sea is made possible by vision, while hearing registers the movement of the waves as music, the implication is that the unity of such reflective perception—aesthetic experience—is the condition of possibility for the unity of nature: the perceiver is not only included in that unity, but produces it as well.

This is the world of "Correspondences," wherein the mingling of scents, sounds, and colors is gathered "In a tenebrous and profound unity / Vast as night and as clarity"—a unity of the riven ideal, of midnight and noon, where Void finally enters into harmony with Soul, World, and God. That harmony requires a metaphysical leap from aesthetic judgment to teleological judgment, such that phenomena themselves would "sing the transports of spirit and sense" across the passage between the finite and the infinite, amid the riddling symbols of their secret identity.

Jean-Pierre Richard tells us that, in *Les Fleurs du Mal*, "it is one of the consequences of the universal law of analogy that between words and things there is no divorce, nor even interval."[94]

---

93 FE, 80-81.

94 Jean-Pierre Richard, *Poésie et Profondeur* (Paris: Éditions de Seuil, 1955), 159. My translation.

And for Émile Benveniste, among many others, the doctrine of correspondences is the alpha and omega of Baudelaire's vision. "Je crois que *correspondance* est le mot-clé de sa poétique"[95] ("I believe that *correspondence* is the keyword of his poetics"), writes Benveniste. In a note titled "Fondement de la poétique baudelairienne" he avows:

> Toute l'attitude de Baudelaire à l'égard du monde, de la vie, de l'homme trouve son unité dans ce principe: *Baudelaire veut mettre en correspondance et en harmonie la nature du monde et la nature de l'homme.*
>
> —
>
> The whole attitude of Baudelaire with regard to the world, to life, to man finds its unity in this principle: *Baudelaire wants to set the nature of the world and the nature of man in correspondence and in harmony.*[96]

In his next note Benveniste sets out the consequences of this view, to his credit, with uncompromising clarity:

> Chez Baudelaire il n'y a pas d'objets. Les choses n'existent pas pour elles- mêmes. Elles ne sont données que par et pour les sentiments qu'elles suscitent en l'homme c'est a dire encore pour les ‹dans leurs› correspondances. Ainsi, les pierres, les métaux — et la beauté féminine — le mouvement des flots et celui de l'âme.
>
> —
>
> In Baudelaire there *are no objects*. Things do not exist for themselves. They are given only by and for the sentiments they arouse in man / that is to say once more in their

---

[95] Émile Benveniste, *Baudelaire*, ed. Chloé Laplantine (Limoges: Éditions Lambert-Lucas, 2011), 282.

[96] Benveniste, *Baudelaire*, 570.

correspondences. Thus, stones, metals — and feminine beauty — the movement of the waves and that of the soul.[97]

Benveniste's verdict is that Baudelaire is a phenomenological and teleological idealist, and it is in this sense that "correspondences" is the "keyword" to his work: there are no objects, things are nothing other than the sentiments to which they give rise, and the telos of poetry is therefore to create the harmony of man and nature.

The lesson Baudelaire draws from his own work, recorded toward the end of the final poem in *Les Fleurs du Mal*, is rather less encouraging:

> Amer savoir, celui qu'on tire du voyage!
> Le monde, monotone et petit, aujourd'hui,
> Hier, demain, toujours, nous fait voir notre image:
> Une oasis d'horreur dans un désert d'ennui!
>
> —
>
> Bitter knowledge, that one draws from the voyage!
> The world, monotonous and small, today,
> Yesterday, tomorrow, always, makes us see our own image:
> An oasis of horror in a desert of ennui![98]

Here we do indeed find "man" reflected by the world through which he travels ("makes us see our own image"), but the only harmony we find in that image is of horror and ennui. Rather than a mirage, we find a real oasis, but it was not the one from which we were hoping to drink. However enthusiastic Baudelaire may be about the doctrine of correspondences in his prose writings, his book is far too at odds with itself and with the world, far too excoriating in its irony to satisfy itself with any doctrine whatsoever. Even if we conceded that Baudelaire

---

97 Benveniste, *Baudelaire*, 572.
98 FE, 452-453.

desires to bring man and world into harmony, he represents the harmony we *actually* find as an oasis of horror in a desert of ennui, and then he represents desire itself as a Siren song, its fulfillment as a deceptive drug:

>   Nous nous embarquerons sur la mer des Ténèbres
>   Avec le coeur joyaux d'un jeune passager.
>   Entendez-vous ces voix charmantes et funèbres,
>   Qui chantent: « Par ici vous qui voulez manger
>
>   « Le Lotus parfumé! c'est ici qu'on vendage
>   Les fruits miraculeux dont votre coeur a faim;
>   Venez-vous enivrer de la douceur étrange
>   De cette après-midi qui n'a jamais de fin? »
>
>   —
>
>   We will load ourselves onto the sea of Shadows
>   With the joyful heart of a youthful passenger.
>   Can you hear those voices, charming and funereal
>   Which sing: "This way those who would eat
>
>   "The scented Lotus! it is here that one harvests
>   The miraculous fruits for which your heart hungers;
>   Won't you drink of the exotic ease
>   Of this afternoon that will never end?"[99]

If it's fine to fall asleep while reading *Les Fleurs du Mal*, we also want to let it wake us up. If we don't want to drift off forever, lulled by the song it both sings and warns us against, we will have to tie ourselves to the mast and decline the scented Lotus.

It is a difficult problem, the question of objects. In a sense it is nearly tautological to say that there are no objects "chez Baudelaire." There are signifiers that refer to objects, and, though it matters that these are themselves objects, it is true

---

[99] FE, 452-453.

that there are no jewels in Baudelaire, only references to jewels. Their "bright and mocking jangle" creates a "luminous world of metal and stone" which "ravishes me in ecstasy," such that "I am furiously in love with / Things wherein sound and light are mingled."[100] Things are beloved for their qualities, and the erasure of *objects* by the *sentiments* they arouse is ravishing. But the ecstasy of this phenomenological idealism, the furious love it inspires, is not straightforwardly affirmed but rather represented as temptation—a seduction to which one gives way at one's own peril. This is the irony of the experience of beauty: it is disinterested, and yet seductive. Baudelaire will lead us through a dialectic in which the beautiful mingling of finite qualities gives rise to a dream of infinite correspondences, itself a kind of seduction, which is doubled by forms of erotic attachment riven by irony. On the one hand, desire draws us toward the land of the perfumed Lotus; on the other hand, it leads to disenchantment.

We find intimations of this irony even in so innocent a quatrain as that which opens "Evening Harmony":

Voici venir les temps où vibrant sur sa tige
Chaque fleurs s'évapore ainsi qu'un encensoir;
Les sons et les parfums tournent dans l'air du soir;
Valse mélancholique et langoureux vertige!

—

Comes the time when stirring on its stem
Every flower diffuses itself like a censer;
Sounds and scents turn in the evening air;
Melancholy waltz and languorous vertigo![101]

100 FE, 104-107.
101 FE, 178-179.

The languor of correspondences amounts to *vertigo*; the waltz of mingling qualities is *melancholic*. Perhaps in this sense Benveniste is right: melancholia involves the introjection of ambivalent attachment to a *lost* object. Is the absence of objects the source of the melancholy called Spleen? Insofar as it requires the displacement of determining judgment by reflective judgment, and thus the displacement of the object by the sentiments it arouses, the experience of beauty is a melancholy waltz. But this waltz is vertiginous because it is danced on fragile footing: to sustain the experience of beauty we must linger within its self-sufficiency, but insofar as we *want* to sustain that satisfaction—insofar as we want to *have it*—we are potentially seduced by the lassitude of lingering and by desire for the possession of what cannot be possessed. Beauty gives rise to desires incompatible with the advent of aesthetic experience.

The desire to *linger* with the beautiful is a form of attachment. In that respect, *pace* Kant, it cannot but involve a pathologically conditioned element of yearning. What do we yearn for, in lingering, if not the plenitude of an experience saturated by the fullness of time? It is the desire for *immersion* in beauty that borders upon intoxication and that lends its experience the lure of oblivion. In *Les Fleurs du Mal* the sexual lure of such intoxication is exoticized, rendered as the plenitude of the elsewhere and the elsewhere of plenitude:

> La langoureuse Asie et la brûlante Afrique,
> Tout un monde lointain, absent, presque défunt,
> Vit dans tes profondeurs, forêt aromatique!
> Comme d'autres esprits voguent sur la musique,
> Le mien, ô mon amour! nage sur ton parfum.

> Languorous Asia and feverish Africa,
> A whole distant world, absent, nearly extinguished,
> Lives in your depths, fragrant forest!
> As other spirits drift upon music,
> My own, o my love! swims upon your perfume.[102]

Music, the passion of other spirits, is distinguished from perfume, the passion of the poet, but the poem is the medium of their synaesthesia, of the immediacy of a distant world: it is in the world of the poem that the scent of the hair can be here and elsewhere, while the distinction is sustained by grammar. The poem is the medium of an orientalist displacement, where presence is rendered as absence, the historical distance of the "nearly extinguished" is found in the contemporary proximity of spatial depth:

> Je plongerai ma tête amoureuse d'ivresse
> Dans ce noir océan où l'autre est enfermé;
> Et mon esprit subtil que le roulis caresse
> Saura vous retrouver, ô féconde paresse,
> Infinis bercements du loisir embaumé!
>
> —
>
> I shall plunge my head enamored of intoxication
> In this black ocean where the other is enclosed;
> And my subtle spirit caressed by the swells
> Will recover you, o fecund indolence,
> Infinite cradlings of balmy leisure!

Féconde paresse, infinis bercements, loisir embaumé: here we have the desire to linger in the experience of the beautiful, distilled to its essence, but grasped as an intoxication at once repressed by and constitutive of the aesthetic. Without such intoxication, how would the displacement of determining

[102] FE, 110-113.

judgment by reflecting judgment take place? If it is a *minimal* intoxication—a *merely formal* intoxication—then Baudelaire's brilliant maneuver is to expand that *mere* into maximal indistinction from Dionysian frenzy, while somehow retaining its mereness. It is indeed the minimum of sensible desire, since it emerges from a mere glimmer. But it attains a maximum of sensual desire, a plenitude, through the mingling of those merely fleeting qualities, a mingling within and through which one wants to linger for an indefinite duration, until one finally finds oneself swooning into fecund indolence, embalming leisure.

Baudelaire does not merely posit but *constructs* this mutation of the aesthetic—within the specificity of the aesthetic—with patient precision. Perhaps it is the major achievement of his authorship, the point of its most implacable singularity, and the major tropic ideology through which he constructs that mutation is orientalism. The poems have to draw the *other* of the aesthetic *into* the aesthetic. Baudelaire writes at the apogee of orientalism's ideological intricacies, at the crux of its structure, and perhaps affirmations of the doctrine of "Correspondences" as the essence of his poetry are a way to linger within the intoxication of "La Chevelure" without dragging in its orientalist baggage. How else could one explain the forgetting (the repression) of the *irony* of the book and thus the bad faith such doctrinal affirmations entail—not least when they issue from Baudelaire? "Correspondences" imports the cargo of such disavowal as "amber, musc, benjamin and incense," without making a spectacle of its origins.

The poem following "La Chevelure" drives home the dialectic of the aesthetic:

> Je t'adore à l'égal de la voûte nocturne,
> Ô vase de tristesse, ô grande taciturne,
> Et t'aime d'autant plus, belle, que tu me fuis,
> Et que tu me parais, ornement de mes nuits,
> Plus ironiquement accumuler les lieues
> Qui séparent mes bras des immensités bleues.

> Je m'avance à l'attaque, et je grimpe aux assauts,
> Comme après un cadavre un choeur de vermisseaux,
> Et je chéris, ô bête implacable et cruelle!
> Jusqu'à cette froideur par où tu m'es plus belle!
>
> —
>
> I adore you even as the nocturnal vault,
> O vase of sadness, o vast reticence,
> And I love you the more, beauty, that you flee from me,
> And that you seem, ornament of my nights,
> More ironically to accumulate the leagues
> That separate my arms from blue immensities.
>
> I launch the attack, and I mount the assault,
> Like a choir of maggots after a cadaver,
> And I cherish, o beast implacable and cruel!
> Even this coldness that increases your beauty![103]

The last two lines recapitulate the relation of courtly love to aesthetic judgment: coldness and cruelty increase beauty, and are thus cherished. The previous line—"Like a choir of maggots after a cadaver"—is rather less conventional, though it bespeaks the nature of the convention more clearly. Isn't this at the core of what Baudelaire does? He has a strange capacity to defamiliarize ideology even as he remains under its spell. In Baudelaire, orientalism and misogyny are what they always were, for the first time. "To the bottom of the Unknown to discover the *new*!"—just like that. The flight of beauty from love is the same as ever, but *more* ironic; it separates as it accumulates, it decomposes as composed. "A choir of maggots after a cadaver" may indeed evoke the harmony of man and nature, but it is a harmony only a necrophiliac could idealize. Such is the history of poetic courtship. It is because Baudelaire not only participates

---

103 FE, 114-115.

in but diagnoses this pathology that it is attributed to him in particular. His candor is disconcerting.

"Une Charogne" returns us to the relation between object and sentiment:

> Oui! telle vous serez, ô la reine des grâces,
>   Aprés les derniers sacrements,
> Quand vous irez, sous l'herbe et les floraisons grasses,
>   Moisir parmi les ossements.
>
> Alors, ô ma beauté! dites à la vermine
>   Qui vous mangera de baisers,
> Que j'ai gardé la forme et l'essence divine
>   De mes amours décomposés!
>
> —
>
> Yes! such you will be, o queen of the graces,
>   After the last rites,
> When you go, below grass and unctuous flowers,
>   To molder among the bones.
>
> Then, o my beauty! say to the vermin
>   Who will devour you with kisses,
> That I saved the form and the essence divine
>   Of my lovers decomposed![104]

The beautiful beloved is the queen of the graces, worshipped by the vermin who devour her, moldering among the bones. But Baudelaire is not among "Those who don't grasp, lovers drunken with flesh, / The nameless elegance of human armature,"[105] so the double irony of these de-idealizing verses is that they are not sarcastic, but sincere. Form and essence really are saved by the composition of decomposition. Yet the point is that there is

104 FE, 126-129.
105 FE, 326-331.

also an obdurate materiality to the form and the essence that are saved. Benveniste refers us to "stones, metals — and feminine beauty — the movement of the waves and that of the soul" as exemplary of things given only for the sentiments they arouse in man, but Baudelaire thinks through the proximity of feminine beauty to stones and metals a little too closely for that kind of comfort. He meditates on the stony objecthood of the soul. Thus he saves the form and essence of his lovers, of love, by insisting that *there are* objects, that things do exist for themselves, and that we are those objects, those things—that the movement of the soul is not only composed but decomposed. To really encounter the sentiments given by things, one has to feel not only the sentiment but the separation of thing from sentiment, to make not only the sentiment but the separation felt. The lines are indeed sincere, but if they were *only* sincere—even as beauty molders among the bones, essence and form are saved by lyric sentiment—they would lose their sting. They also have to be sarcastic. Irony is the unity of sarcasm and sincerity; this unity is ironic.

These reflections lead us toward the encounter of lyric idealization with the irrevocable materiality of the body, which survives the soul as the bone of spirit. It is on an ideal island where that encounter will take place, for Baudelaire's irony does not spare his own colonial fantasies of a beautiful, feminized elsewhere, retained in memory and dreamed in imagination. The port is a locus wherein the traces of sensory qualities, like the fragrance of perfume, mingle with corporeal intimations of tropical distances:

> Guidé par ton odeur vers de charmants climats,
> Je vois un port rempli de voiles et de mâts
> Encor tout fatigués par la vague marine,

> Pendant que le parfum des verts tamariniers,
> Qui circule dans l'air et m'enfle la narine,
> Se mêle dans mon âme au chant des mariniers.
>
> —
>
> Guided by your scent toward charming climes,
> I see a port replete with sails and masts
> Still wearied by the tossing sea,
>
> While the perfume of green tamarinds,
> That circles in the air and swells in the nostril,
> Mingles in my soul with the mariners' song.[106]

The synaesthesia of sensible qualities is replete with historical circumstance, such that the scent of "Exotic Perfume" is at once that of a balmy breast ("ton sein chaleureux") and of green tamarinds from

> Une île paresseuse où la nature donne
> Des arbres singuliers et des fruits savoureux;
> Des homme dont le corps est mince et vigoureux,
> Et des femmes dont l'oeil par sa franchise étonne.
>
> —
>
> An indolent island where nature offers
> Curious trees and savory fruits;
> Men of slender and vigorous build,
> And women with eyes of startling candor.

The port is a synthetic site, linking the presence of the exotic mistress with the absence of an exotic island, establishing a sensory relay between here and elsewhere. The imagination—both synthesis of the sensible and synthesis of the subject—mediates between body and mind, nostril and soul, such that the soul is

---

106 FE, 108-109.

mingled with the mariners' song through circulation. As goods circulate through the port, the scent circles in evanescent air, is absorbed by corporeal olfactory receptors, and mingles the soul with the intersubjectivity of song.

It is the mingling of the aesthetic and the historical that is indexed by the relay between sensory singularity and colonial fantasy. Earlier we understood those elements of anguished resentment in the tenebrous mistress poems in terms of a failed mitigation of the absolute, the impossibility of figuring the void through *mélange*. Here we can understand the symptoms of historical repression we find in those poems in terms of the pressure of history upon aesthetic experience. That pressure is both desired and disavowed, loved and hated not only because it suggests the repressed violence of colonial revery, but also because of the *poetic* difficulty of including history within the beautiful, given the disinterest of the aesthetic to normativity. Yet this pressure comes to the foreground in "A Voyage to Cythera," anchoring the section titled "Fleurs du Mal" in both the 1857 and 1861 editions. It is in this poem that the dialectic we have been following through its circumnavigations arrives at a confrontation with its contradictions, right at the crux of history and beauty, on an island where we find the violence of the Ideal.

The poem sets out amid "les minutes heureuses."[107] We are along for the voyage to which we were previously invited, aboard a ship bound for the indolent island where Venus rose from the sea:

Mon coeur, comme un oiseau, voltigeait tout joyeux
Et planait librement à l'entour des cordages;
La navire roulait sous un ciel sans nuages,
Comme un ange enivré d'un soleil radieux.

---

107 FE, 144-147.

My heart, like a bird, fluttered joyfully
And hovered freely around the ropes;
The ship swayed beneath a cloudless sky,
Like an angel drunk on radiant sun.[108]

A drunken angel is the figure of the intoxication of the beautiful—pure, yet made sensual by purity, swaying in a radiant light proximate to that evoked in the closing quatrains of "Benediction," which are spoken in the voice of the Poet both damned and elect:

« Mais les bijoux perdus de l'antique Palmyre,
Les métaux inconnus, les perles de la mer,
Par votre main montés, ne pourraient pas suffire
A ce beau diadème éblouissant et clair;

« Car il ne sera fait que de pure lumière,
Puisée au foyer sant des rayon primitifs,
Et dont les yes mortels, dans leur splendeur entière,
Ne sont que des miroirs obscurcise et plaintifs! »

—

"But the vanished jewels of ancient Palmyra,
The undiscovered metals, the pearls of the sea,
By your own hand set, could never suffice
For this beautiful diadem dazzling and clear;

For it will be made of pure light,
Drawn from the holy hearth of pristine rays,
Of which mortal eyes, in all their splendor,
Are but obscure and mournful mirrors!"[109]

---

[108] FE, 406-411.
[109] FE, 50-55.

In "Benediction," the light is truly Ideal, "drawn from the holy hearth of pristine rays" and crowning the Poet with a *metaphysical* diadem, dazzling and clear, superior even to unknown precious metals, to pearls of the abyssal depths, to the shrouded gem of "Le Guignon." The mortal eyes of finite beings are but mournful mirrors of such infinitely pure light. Yet "the vanished jewels of ancient Palmyra" are called upon as that light's most proximate analogue, that which must be exceeded by hyperbole, and this *comparison* constitutes the poetic ground of the ineffable. It is *ground* which is at stake in these lines of "Benediction": the evocation of the divine absolute is constructed through relation—as we saw was inevitable in the case of the absolute void—and this relational construction itself is the *poetic* inscription of the absolute, which therefore becomes relative. "But," "could never suffice," "For it will be made," "are but": this is the grammar of poetic determination, the grammar of relation, of qualification, negation, entailment, delimitation. The diadem of the poet is "made of pure light," but the poem forges that assertion of the absolute through the grammar of the relative and through the figural differentials to which it gives rise. The jewels of ancient Palmyra, themselves beautiful to contemplate, enter the poem by way of their *exclusion* from the Poet's diadem: they are insufficient to the Poet's crown but they suffice for its description in the poem. The poem is not what it says: what it says is that the absolute is pure light, that this is the essence of poetry, the crown of the Poet. Yet the poem *is* a differential texture of relation, since in order to be included in the poem—"ce beau diademe"—the absolute must not only be thought or asserted, but made.

In "Benediction" this lesson is implicit: poetry requires a logic of relation that must be limned amid the evocation of the pure absolute, those "rayons primitif" which crown the Poet. Due to this discrepancy between the *making* of poetry and the immateriality of the Poet's crown, he will be dragged down to earth. The de-idealizing consequences of these implications are made explicit in the second strophe of "Voyage to Cythera," where the joyful heart encounters, in the field of vision, its seduction by cliché and hyperbole:

> Quelle est cette île triste et noire? — C'est Cythère,
> Nous dit-on, un pays fameux dans les chansons,
> Eldorado banal de tous les vieux garçons.
> Regardez, après tout, c'est une pauvre terre.
>
> —
>
> What is this island sad and black? — It is Cythera,
> They say, a country renown in songs,
> Banal Eldorado of old men everywhere.
> Look, after all, it's a pitiful place.

Note the absence of negation. When the absolute is evoked, as in "Benediction," we are told what could *never suffice* to attain it. When we encounter the reality of what songs have made famous, our disenchantment can be flatly stated: "c'est une pauvre terre." And yet, listen to how lovely is the simple sound of the realization: — *C'est Cythère*. Poetry enchants as it disenchants. Such is the lure of "Correspondences": a dialectic may be taken for a doctrine. But poetry undoes the doctrinal.[110] The Cythera of lore is a banal Eldorado. Its celebration in song is a *langage connu*. "Regardez, après tout": after all, we see the poor world that had been represented as the harmonious temple of Nature. The rhetoric here recalls "Heutontimoroumenos"—"Ne suis-je pas un faux accord / Dans la divine symphonie?"[111] It is the rhetoric of dawning realization, the insistent nag of the ineradicable

---

110 As Claude Pichois writes in his notes on "Correspondances," "Le poète en use selon son privilège: tout est matière à poésie; la poèsie est irréductible à l'histoire des idées. Le poète n'adhère pas à une doctrine." ("The poet uses it according to his privilege: everything is poetic material; poetry is irreducible to the history of ideas. The poet does not adhere to any doctrine.") Baudelaire, *Oeuvres Complètes* I, 843.

111 FE 270-273.

question, the dreadful query to which one already knows the answer, "Quelle est cette île...." It is because the I is *un faux accord* that, after all, we can learn to recognize the voracious Irony of the world in which we actually live. If there is to be a symphony in the wake of that recognition, it will have to be one that is not divinely harmonious, yet not banal either—a dissonant symphony in which false chords may be heard without thereby integrating them into a higher harmony. Since poetry enchants as it disenchants, it lures us toward the isle of the scented Lotus even as it warns that we will find a pitiful place. So, without subsuming it back into teleological harmony, we have to hold onto our registration of disenchantment as a persistent discord within the aesthetic, even as poetry makes that discord undeniably beautiful—*C'est Cythère / c'est une pauvre terre*.

Look at how the poem then proceeds through the following three quatrains, repeating and expanding the opposition of the first two while rounding out its introductory movement and arriving at a glimpse of the singular object that will consume our attention thereafter:

— Île des doux secrets et des fêtes du coeur!
De l'antique Vénus le superbe fantôme
Au-dessus de tes mers plane comme un arôme,
Et charge les esprits d'amour et de langueur.

Belle île aux myrtes verts, pleine de fleurs écloses,
Vénérée à jamais par toute nation,
Où les soupirs des coeurs en adoration
Roulent comme l'encens sur un jardin de roses

Ou le roucoulement éternel d'un ramier!
— Cythère n'était plus qu'un terrain des plus maigres,
Un désert rocailleux troublé par des cris aigres.
J'entrevoyais pourtant un objet singulier!

—

— Isle of sweet secrets and heart's revels!
The glorious ghost of ancient Venus
Hovers over your seas like a scent,
And fills our spirits with love and languor.

Beautiful isle of green myrtle, full of flowers in bloom,
Venerated for all time by every nation,
Where the sighs of hearts in adoration
Waft like incense through a garden of roses

Or the eternal cooing of a dove!
—Cythera was no more than the most meager of lands,
A stony desert strafed by stringent cries.
Yet I caught a glimpse of a singular object!

Having confronted the poor place, we turn back to the imagination of what it once was, to the superb phantom of antiquity. The hovering aroma is like that which mingles the soul with the mariner's song in "Exotic Perfume," filling our spirits with love and languor: the love of the beautiful that makes us linger within its advent. Thus we give leave to the dream of what is not the case, as though it once were, transporting the severance of reality from expectation over to the severance between the present and the past, so as to preserve the possibility of perfect beauty by consigning it to history and thereby (paradoxically) clearing it of history and its conflicts: Cythera *was* "Vénérée à jamais par toute nation." Yet again, the poem proves it is possible for beauty to exist here and now, just through something so simple as a description of what isn't there, though the apparent simplicity belies days consumed in austere study. "Belle île aux myrtes verts": it is the cramped piquancy of "myrtes vert," the sharpness of the *y* meeting the *t* across the pause of the *r*, the way the repetition of the *r* in "verts" slows us down at the hemistich, which counterpoints the lovely openness of sound and sense in "pleine de fleurs écloses." Here the imagination of a cliché is described with a cliché (blooming flowers), but the sound of the description is not a cliché; it is the redemption of cliché by beauty. The gift of the poem is the immanence of that redemption to language; one's mouth becomes beautiful just by forming the sounds of beauty's ruin, and then we find that ruin itself amid the syllables, stony and stringent as what they describe: "Un désert rocailleux troublé par des cris aigres." Through this description of what *was* the case (in the mind) and what *is* the case now (in the flesh), we are prepared for the center of the poem. What is this singular object of which the speaker has caught a glimpse?

But before we find out, we get one more glimpse of what it is not. Creeping into the poem through the ghostliness of the past ("Cythère n'était plus"), the logic of negation now grants us one more quatrain's reprieve before we are given to see a corpse on a gibbet, disemboweled, enucleated, castrated, and devoured by ferocious birds:

> Ce n'était pas un temple aux ombres bocagères,
> Où la jeune prêtresse, amoureuse des fleurs,
> Allait, le corps brûlé de secrètes chaleurs,
> Entrebâillant sa robe aux brises passagères.

> It was not a temple amid shady groves,
> Where a young priestess, lover of flowers,
> Went, her body inflamed by secret fervors,
> Slipping open her robe for passing breezes;

The object we will see does *not*, in other words, belong to the world of "Correspondences"—it was not "a temple amid shady groves." Perhaps there used to be a priestess whose innocent love of flowers made her body burn with eros. Again, we are given to imagine the beauty of a disappeared or mythic past. But the third line already intimates what we are about to encounter, "le corps brûlé." What *it was not* secretly suggests what *it is*, such that *there is* a correspondence, but through a brutally bitter, painful, nearly unthinkable relation, rather than a harmonious synthesis.

Ce n'était pas...Mais voilà: finally the poem gets to the point, which is horror. Baudelaire insists that there is at least *one* object in his book ("un objet singulier!"), a gibbet suspending the corpse of a hanged man. In fact, the word "objet" is used four times in *Les Fleurs du Mal*, with revealing consistency:

Aux objets répugnants nous trouvons des appas;[112]

...

Rappelez-vous l'objet que nous vîmes, mon âme[113]

...

Parmi les objets noirs ou roses
Qui composent son corps charmant,[114]

...

J'entrevoyais pourtant un objet singulier![115]

Once it refers to a gibbet, once to a carrion, once to unspecified repugnant objects in which we discover charms, and once it refers to discrete parts composing a female body. In this last case, The Demon tempts a lover to choose the sweetest among all the things comprising his enchantment, and the lover replies by launching into a hymn to the exquisite harmony of his beloved's beautiful body, which must be idolized "Tout Entière." This is a correct reply to the Demon, if one doesn't want to be caught at fault. But whenever *the object* is at issue in *Les Fleurs du Mal*, it is a matter of death, decomposition, repugnance, or reification. The objecthood of the gibbet is clearly outlined—"Du ciel se

---

112 FE, 44.
113 FE, 126.
114 FE, 160.
115 FE, 406.

détachant en noir, comme un cyprès"—as if to insist that it remain unabsorbed. It will be designated as a "symbol" in the poem's final strophe, "un gibet symbolique," but it matters that this symbol is also "un objet singulier." In order to be *this* symbol, it must retain its objecthood, detached from the sky in black. It is a symbol of death, "comme un cyprès," and not a symbol of resurrection, like a cross. It is a symbol of objecthood itself, which is what it must mean to be a singular object.

What we thus encounter on the gibbet is not thing-become-sentiment, but sentiment-become-thing:

> De féroces oiseaux perchés sur leur pâture
> Détruisaient avec rage un pendu déjà mûr,
> Chacun plantant, comme un outil, son bec impur
> Dans tous les coins saignants de cette pourriture;
>
> Les yeux étaient deux trous, et du ventre effondré
> Les intestins pesants lui coulaient sur les cuisses,
> Et ses bourreaux, gorgés de hideuses délices,
> L'avaient à coups de bec absolument châtré.

—

> Ferocious birds perched upon their prey
> Destroying with rage a ripe hanged man,
> Each driving, like a spade, its filthy beak
> Into every bleeding recess of rot;
>
> The eyes were two holes, and from the eroded belly
> Heavy intestines poured down the thighs,
> And his torturers, gorged upon gruesome delights,
> Had pecked him absolutely castrated.

The rhyme scheme nearly collapses in the first strophe. Monorhyme is held off only through the minimal difference between *ure* and *ur*—an erosion of form as the birds drive their beaks into every bleeding recess of the body. The destiny of the unburied body is annihilation rather than veneration; the ceremony of rhyme gives way to a stutter. Since the beaks are like spades digging into the corpse, the corpse itself is like a grave. Unburied, it *is* the hole in which it does not lie.

The condition of *being* a grave rather than *having* a grave inverts the logic of castration, which is crucial to the poem. The psychic figure of the phallus involves an unconscious dialectic of being and having that is bound up with desire: since having a certain kind of body—any body whatever—does not amount to having the phallus, one either *tries to have it* or *tries to be it*. The threat of castration is that of losing what one *wants* to have (the phallus) or *wants* to be ("a man"). But the *materiality* of castration is another matter: it is not a question of desire or threat, but of embodied fact. The violence of castration is the reduction of the body to an object through the localization of its symbolic dignity (spirit) in one *part* of the body, which is removed. The horror of castration is that the penis actually becomes the phallus—and this is only possible through its negation. Through a metonymic simile ("comme un outil"), Baudelaire radicalizes the implications of this structure in its specific application to a corpse: a castrated corpse, unburied, is a grave. This would be what it means to be *absolutely* castrated ("absolument châtré"). The body is not only reduced to an object, but to the object-form of nothing. This is what we see on the island of Cythera, where Aphrodite rose from the foam of a sky god's discarded genitals. Such is the birth of love, since whatever embodied forms it takes, love is bound by the dialectic of being and having. Here that dialectic is reduced to its terrible ground, a stony desert strafed with stringent cries.

Yet the concluding movement of the poem begins by paying tribute to this negative remainder of the cult of love and beauty, recognized as the true inhabitant of Cythera:

> Habitant de Cythère, enfant d'un ciel si beau,
> Silencieusement tu souffrais ces insultes
> En expiation de tes infâmes cultes
> Et des péchés qui t'ont interdit le tombeau.

—

> Inhabitant of Cythera, child of so beautiful a sky,
> Silently you suffered these insults
> In expiation of your cultic infamies
> And of sins that forbade you the tomb.

Baudelaire derives the scenario from Nerval's travel writings, which figure the discrepancy between his dream of Cythera and the reality of the island as a veritable flight of the gods. Nerval records his sudden recognition of an object, at first mistaken for the statue of a divine protectress, as a gibbet with three branches, "only one of which was garnished." "The first real gibbet I had ever seen," he writes; "it was on the soil of Cythera, English possession, that I was given to see it."[116] Following Nerval's description, Baudelaire represents the destroyed corpse as that of a native inhabitant of the island punished for pagan practices by British colonists. The mutilated "Habitant de Cythère" is thus a remnant of the pagan world tortured, killed, and forbade a tomb by Christians during the century of the death of God—the symbol of both a fallen ancient world and the horror of a desacralized colonial modernity.

The speaker then addresses the corpse directly and, with wrenching sincerity, invokes the name of the Lord to plead for strength and courage:

---

116 Nerval in *L'Artiste*, August 11, 1844, quoted in Pichois and Dupont, eds., *L'Atelier de Baudelaire*, Tome I, 596. My translation.

Ridicule pendu, tes douleurs sont les miennes!
Je sentis, à l'aspect de tes membres flottants,
Comme un vomissement, remonter vers mes dents
Le long fleuve de fiel des douleurs anciennes;

Devant toi, pauvre diable au souvenir si cher,
J'ai senti tous les becs et toutes les mâchoires
Des corbeaux lancinants et des panthères noires
Qui jadis aimaient tant à triturer ma chair.

— Le ciel était charmant, la mer était unie;
Pour moi tout était noir et sanglant désormais,
Hélas! et j'avais, comme en un suaire épais,
Le coeur enseveli dans cette allégorie.

Dans ton île, ô Vénus! je n'ai trouvé debout
Qu'un gibet symbolique où pendait mon image.....
— Ah! Seigneur! donnez-moi la force et le courage
De contempler mon coeur et mon corps sans dégoût!

—

Ridiculous hanged man, your sufferings are mine!
I feel, at the sight of your swaying limbs,
Like vomit, that rises toward my teeth
The long river of bile flow from ancient pains;

There before you, poor devil in memory held dear,
I felt every beak and every jaw
Of the thrusting crows and the black panthers
Who once so loved to grind my flesh.

— The sky was lovely, the sea was smooth;
For me all was black and bloody hereafter,
Alas! for I had, as in a thick shroud,
Buried my heart in this allegory.

> On your island, o Venus, I found nothing left
> But a symbolic gibbet where my image was hung.....
> — Ah! Lord! give me the strength and the courage
> To look without loathing upon my body and my heart!

Allegory, symbol, image: the whole problem of Baudelaire's poetry is at stake in this poem. Our claim is that it is the problem of poetic determination. Baudelaire not only identifies with the suffering of the corpse, he determines it as his image. He determines the gibbet as the symbol from which his image is suspended, and he determines the whole complex of the poem—the relation between the fantasy of the ancient and the reality of the modern—as the allegory in which his heart is buried. Allegory thus marks the *difference* between the speaker and the corpse with which he identifies: the corpse is unburied, but the poet's heart is buried in the allegory of the unburied corpse, "as in a thick shroud." Image and symbol take the cruelty of history and the materiality of suffering into the world of the poem; they poeticize it without idealizing it. The absolutely determined body gives rise to the determination of the speaker "To look without loathing upon my body and my heart." Here the dialectic of poetic determination reaches a non-teleological terminus. We cannot say that the poem, considered as a whole, is beautiful—that would be to erase a horror unassimilable by the aesthetic, which gives the poem its power. What is beautiful in the poem is sustained alongside, but does not cancel, the ruin of beauty that it records. Here, allegory includes what beauty could never include, in its disharmony *with* beauty, and the ambition articulated in the final line is at once minimal and colossal: for who among us has been able to achieve it? To look without loathing is not to reclaim the rites of the cult of beauty, but to settle for something apparently beneath its dignity: the capacity to face the worst, to know it as oneself, and to bear the recognition. Confronted with the limit of *being determined* (the corpse), the speaker *determines* to bear the actuality of his own body, of his own heart—or at least, he asks for the strength to do so. That is the poem's allegory of determination. It is crucial that when the speaker calls upon the Lord for courage and strength he interpellates himself not only as tortured heretic but also as Christian persecutor. All the religion (travestied) that Baudelaire put in his atrocious book is found right here.

In "A Voyage to Cythera," enchantment turns to horror. "The Little Old Ladies" reverses this trajectory:

> Dans les plis sinueux des vieilles capitales,
> Où tout, même l'horreur, tourne aux enchantements,
> Je guette, obéissant à mes humeurs fatales,
> Des êtres singuliers, décrépits et charmants.[117]

—

> In the sinuous folds of old capitals,
> Where all, even horror, turns to enchantment,
> I spy, obeying my fatal humors,
> Certain singular beings, decrepit and charming.

Now horror will turn to enchantment, by virtue of an endearing voyeurism. This is a poem about looking and following ("Ah! que j'en ai suivi de ces petites vieilles!"), about how to look without loathing not at oneself but at other singular beings, and about how to obey one's own fate—how to *follow* those fatal humors that make us the singular beings, decrepit and occasionally charming, that we are.

In *Notre-Dame de Paris* Hugo describes the act of following someone through the streets as a "voluntary abdication of one's free will." To follow is "a subjection of one's own fancy to that of some unsuspecting other person," and it involves "a mixture of whimsical independence and blind obedience, a sort of compromise between servitude and freedom."[118] We can recognize

---

117 FE, 304-311.
118 Victor Hugo, *Notre-Dame de Paris*, trans. John Sturrock (New York: Penguin, 1978), 69.

the dialectic of determination at work: the one who follows *determines* to be *determined*. The speaker of "Lethe"—who takes "my destiny" as "my delight" and obeys it as predestination—now finds a way beyond the scene of the two that poem entails. There, the lover is determined to poison himself "at the charming tips of this pointed breast" ("Aux bouts charmants de cette gorge aiguë")[119]—a mere reversal of courtly love tropes. Here, it is the charming plurality of singular beings that determines the voyeur's "mixture of whimsical independence and blind obedience," and the beings who are followed are actually granted the grace of singularity.[120] We are in the sinuous folds of the same old city, but also in a totally different world than that of "À Une Passante." There, it is the fleeting glimpse of fugitive beauty, fascinating and deadly, that intoxicates the speaker. Something far more interesting than "shock experience" is at issue in "Les Petites Vieilles." Here we are not left with the fantasy of love at last sight and the projection of what *could have* been. The poem is replete with projection, but it is that of sustained devotion shorn of erotic promise, of observation saturated by social concern, of attention to mysteries stranger than those of what is merely unknown.

As Baudelaire introduces the singular beings of his poem, it is the complexity of his free indirect discourse that catches the eye:

> Ces monstres disloqués furent jadis des femmes,
> Eponine ou Laïs! Monstres brisés, bossus
> Ou tordus, aimons-les! ce sont encor des âmes.
> Sous des jupons troués et sous de froids tissus

---

119 FE, 134-135.

120 On figures of feminine singularity in *Les Fleurs du Mal*, see Ronjaunee Chatterjee's important article, "Baudelaire and Feminine Singularity," *French Studies* 70.1 (January 2016): 17-32.

Ils rampent, flagellés par les bises iniques,
Frémissant au fracas roulant des omnibus,
Et serrant sur leur flanc, ainsi que des reliques,
Un petit sac brodé de fleurs ou de rébus;

Ils trottent, tout pareils à des marionnettes;
Se traînent, comme font les animaux blessés,
Ou dansent, sans vouloir danser, pauvres sonnettes
Où se pend un Démon sans pitié! Tout cassés

Qu'ils sont, ils ont des yeux perçants comme une vrille,
Luisants comme ces trous où l'eau dort dans la nuit;
Ils ont les yeux divins de la petite fille
Qui s'étonne et qui rit à tout ce qui reluit.

—

These disjointed monsters who once were women,
Eponine or Laïs! Broken monsters, hunchbacked
Or twisted, let us love them! they are still ensouled.
Under tattered skirts and flimsy fabrics

They creep, whipped by iniquitous winds,
Trembling amid the omnibus clatter,
And clutching to their hip, as if some relic,
A purse embroidered with flowers or rebus;

They trot, as if they were marionettes;
Limp along, as wounded animals do,
Or dance, without meaning to dance, poor bells
From which dangles some pitiless Demon! Cracked

Though they are, their eyes pierce like a drill,
Gleaming like those holes where water sleeps at night;
Divine eyes like those of the little girl
Who startles and laughs at all that shines.

In the first two lines we shift between the objectifying gaze of a general sociality, the discourse of a careless They who sees only disjointed and broken monsters, hunchbacked or twisted, "who once were women." The reduction of women to monsters, by way of corporeal decrepitude, is broken by the exclamation of legendary names, the names of "Poetry," that likewise reduce singularity to canonical precedent. Both of these discursive registers are then interrupted by a voice at once casual and earnest, good-humored and insistent: "aimons-les! ce sont encor des âmes." Again we might recognize a reversal of "A Voyage to Cythera": singular beings rather than a singular object, beings that are still souls rather than the reduction of the body to spiritless materiality. But the ensouled persistence of these beings comes to include the particularity of their bodies through the insistence of the speaker that they cannot be reduced to it: they *are* disjointed, broken, hunchbacked, and twisted; they *do* wear tattered skirts and flimsy fabrics. In a word, they are not beautiful. So the lingering at issue within the world of the poem, the reflective feeling communicated by the speaker, is not that of the aesthetic. It is normative and moral: let us love them, they are still ensouled. What we want to point out is that this normative discourse is only rescued from banality by the subtle perspectival field of free indirect discourse, by the plural registers of reductive objectification, mythic idealization, calm and gentle recognition. None of these are canceled. They mingle like those sensory singularities that blend within the poems. The task of recognition is not only narrated but also demanded of the reader at the level of interpretation: can we parse the tonalities of the soul that speak through the lines? Which do we identify with? Can we sense our way among particulars toward the singularities of those peculiar beings, so many, whose voices teem in our own brains?

The women *creep* and they *limp* like wounded animals, yet they *trot* like marionettes and they *dance* like bells. Artifice enters along with animality. Hugo's pitiful hunchback makes an implicit appearance, by way of the pitiless Demon dangling from the bell, which, just as we hear it ring out, sings only with the enfeebled voice of "La Cloche Felée." The discourse of the poem folds together the deft enchantments of theater and the fragility of animal bodies with the narrative fantasies of the novel and the intertextual worlds of *Les Fleurs du Mal* itself, speaking through its own poems in the voice of its own otherness. The winds that whip the women are *iniquitous*: nature is charged with normativity insofar as it passes through the polis, whereas the omnibus is just the immediacy of its noise. Relics, flowers, and rebus are united by an embroidered purse, such that religion, craft, logic, and free beauty are clutched together by an object at once bound to the abstract destinies of exchange and so intimate it is practically part of one's body. These are the new flowers of which Baudelaire dreams, in full bloom, and the mystical food that fuels their force is a mastery of poetic implication that was already there at twenty, yet has matured through such intricate traceries of the soul that it cannot be distinguished from what it describes. Whatever it touches upon is stitched into the social field and embroidered with puzzles. And now, in the last of the strophes quoted above, it becomes possible to identify the sleeping water of potholes with the divine eyes of a little girl through the eyes of old women that pierce like a drill. The water gleams, the eyes pierce, the girl startles, the sound of the drill bores into the city as the clatter of the omnibus shakes it, the wounded animals dance, the bells trot, and the marionnettes sing in the voice of a soldier dying under a heap of bodies, while the coins clink softly in the purse as the wind limps along and the iniquitous Demon trembles at the poverty of his pitilessness amid the ensoulment of the world, the meaningless truth of its disjointed tatters come to dwell at last where it has always been, where the water sleeps, sleeps through the night that cracks for those with eyes to see the divine laughter that love is, written, tender in its precision, twisted among flimsy fabrics—can you feel how closely it is clutched to the hip, the possession of what will be paid out, the persistence of those who once were? Look: all that shines is shining. We are here on earth amid the actual, cracked though it is. Now follow its fracture wherever it leads.

Who speaks? What are the limits of free indirect discourse? Where does it begin, and where does it end? We know that we are spoken through by unknown powers and personas, though sometimes their origin is dreadfully, tediously, or charmingly obvious. When we describe something, *how many* are in the description? They speak, sometimes in familiar tones, sometimes in a single voice (which is not mine), sometimes in multiplicities of tenebrous whispers. Sometimes all the living and the dead trail in the trace of a single phrase (*sunt lacrimae rerum et mentum mortalia tangunt*). Sometimes the soulless banality of the univocal They crowds out the possibilities of what could have been said. Gustave Flaubert is an exacting instructor in the deviations of free indirect discourse, the way its narrative movements can unearth the enchantment, the horror, and the everydayness of a world and a voice that never quite belong to us, though we claim them as property. Here is the opening of Part II of *Madame Bovary*, in Lydia Davis's luminous translation:

> You leave the highway at La Boissière and continue level as far as the top of Les Leux hill, from which you first discern the valley. The stream that runs through it creates two regions distinct in physiognomy: everything on the left is in pasture, everything on the right is tillage. The grassland extends under a fold of low hills to join at the far end the pastures of the Bray country, while to the east, the plain, rising gently, broadens out and extends its blond wheat fields as far as the eye can see. The water that runs along the edge of the grass divides with its line of white the color of the meadows from the color of the furrows, so that the countryside resembles a great mantle, unfolded, its green velvet collar edged with silver braid.

On the horizon before you, when you arrive, you have the oaks of the Argueil forest and the escarpments of the Saint-Jean hill, streaked from top to bottom by long, irregular trails of red; these are the marks left by the rains, and their brick-red tones, standing out so clearly in slender threads against the gray of the mountain, come from the abundance of ferruginous springs that flow beyond, in the surrounding countryside.

Here you are on the borders of Normandy, Picardy, and Île-de-France, a mongrel region where the language is without expressive emphasis, just as the landscape is without character. It is here that they make the worst Neufchâtel cheeses in the whole district, while farming is costly, because a good deal of manure is needed to enrich this crumbly soil full of sand and stones.

Until 1835, there was no passable road for reaching Yonville; but at about that time they established a *major local route* that connects the Abbeville road to that of Amiens and is sometimes used by carters going from Rouen to Flanders. Nevertheless, Yonville-l'Abbaye has stood still, despite its *new outlets*. Instead of improving the cultivated lands, the people here persist in maintaining the pastures, however depreciated they may be, and the lazy town, moving away from the plain, has continued naturally to grow toward the river. You can see it from far off, stretched out along the bank, like a cowherd taking his nap at the water's edge.

Directly addressing the reader as a generic "you," this is clearly the discourse of the narrator, not of a character. Or is it? Who is it who says, in the third paragraph, that "the language is without expressive emphasis, just as the landscape is without character"? Who judges the Neufchâtel cheeses to be the worst in the whole district? Is the one who calculates the cost of manure the same one who says that "the countryside resembles a great mantle, unfolded, its green velvet collar edged with silver braid"? Is the one who compares the lazy town to "a cowherd taking his nap at the water's edge" the same one who uses the terms "*major local route*" and "*new outlets*"? Does the voice of capitalist progress—which chastises the inhabitants of Yonville for persisting in maintaining the pastures rather than improving the cultivated lands—come from the same source as the voice of the pastoral poet, who sees the brick-red tones of marks left by the rains as "slender threads against the gray of the mountain"? Through the compound discourse of the narrator, the voice of Monsieur Homais already speaks before we meet him, Emma Bovary already sighs before she arrives in town, and liquid manure already flows before its praises are sung at the Agricultural Fair while Rodolphe pours out his heart to Emma. Yet the voice of morn in russet mantle clad also speaks through the discourse of the narrator, as it walks o'er the dew of yon high eastward hill. What does *lazy* mean? Is that pejorative or affectionate? Is it good or bad to stretch out along the bank? Norms are the shadows of adjectives. Is a sleeping cowherd lazy like a gentle breeze, or lazy like someone who should be making improvements, but isn't? It depends on who "you" are.

The boundary of free indirect discourse, its horizon, is potentially unlimited because all speech and all discourse is social, subtended and infiltrated by ideology, by tradition, by intonations of literature and song, by advertising and parental admonition, such that the voices of discrepant individuals are always latent in the speech of any one person, while the discourse of The Narrator is composed of partially individuated elements of diffuse sociality. The discourse of Baudelaire's "speaker" is an uneven psychological and linguistic surface, marked by rains and streaked with an ideal red whose rusty depth comes from the abundance of ferruginous springs that flow beyond, and it is a fabric woven of slender threads that have themselves been spun of heterogenous filaments. As intricately as any passage in *Les Fleurs du Mal*, the three quatrains forming the second section of "Les Petites Vieilles" display the profound complexity its discourse can communicate:

De Frascati défunt Vestale enamourée;
Prêtresse de Thalie, hélas! dont le souffleur
Enterré sait le nom; célèbre évaporée
Que Tivoli jadis ombragea dans sa fleur,

Toutes m'enivrent! mais parmi ces êtres frêles
Il en est qui, faisant de la douleur un miel,
Ont dit au Dévouement qui leur prêtait ses ailes:
Hippogriffe puissant, mène-moi jusque'au ciel

L'une, par sa patrie au malheur exercée,
L'autre, que son époux surchargea de douleurs,
L'autre, par son enfant Madone transpercée,
Toutes auraient pu faire un fleuve avec leurs pleurs!

—

Vestal beloved of defunct Frascati;
Priestess of Thalia, alas! the buried prompter
Knows the name; evaporated fame
Once shaded by Tivoli in full flower,

All intoxicate; yet among these frail beings
Are those who, turning sadness to honey,
Have said to Devotion who lends them his wings:
Powerful Hippogriff, carry me to heaven!

One, by her country schooled in hardship,
Another, whom her husband has surcharged with sorrow,
Another, by child made transpierced Madonna,
All could have poured out a river of tears!

Realism was to be the burial of Romanticism—is this realist or romantic? It depends on which strophe one is reading. The discourse of the speaker is like the honeybee, unmentioned, which is the vehicle of the central metaphor: it gathers the nectar of sadness from many different flowers and secretes it into a single substance of compound flavor, stored in prismatic cells. In the first quatrain we encounter Roman, Greek, and Renaissance models: a Vestal Virgin, the Priestess of a Muse, a shaded inhabitant of lavish gardens. In the third quatrain, one exercised by country, another abused by marriage, and another suffering the pains of motherhood. All intoxicate and all are in tears. Shifting discursive registers move between a lost past and a painful present, yet what these women have in common is that none are identified by name. In the first quatrain, we seem to be on stage: only "the buried prompter / Knows the name." These are parts that are played—Virgin, Priestess, Aristocrat—and an actor has forgotten the name of the character, while the prompter who would deliver it is long since dead. The speaker of the poem is an actor on a transhistorical stage, and therefore *also* playing a part, while subject to a lapse of memory. Literary styles are roles: they can occupy the same stage, they can enter the same poem through different discursive moods, yet emotions and commitments can also traverse them and the histories from which they emerge. The names of the women are forgotten, but the women remember the name of Devotion, who lends them his wings, thus turning them into honeybees as they, frail beings, turn sadness to honey. Yet as they call upon the mythical Hippogriff to carry them to heaven, the poem returns us to an earth of service and hardship, from honey to tears. These strophes are saturated with images, dreams, and realities of the ancient and the modern, and saturation is the point. The honeycomb is full, the tears pour like a river: poetic discourse is replete with historical, mythical, and existential determination. At the end of the poem's first part, the eyes of the women are described as "wells made of a million tears, / Crucibles spangled by cooling metal..." Every particular, each tear, enters into the water in the well; the molten substance in the crucible is differentiated as glowing spangles, while the heat of composition cools into the metallic solidity of the made poem.

Thanks to the poem's proliferation of figures, determinate finitude gives rise not only to suffering, forgetting, and mortality, but also to captivating symbols and curious riddles:

— Avez-vous observé que maints cercueils de vieilles
Sont presque aussi petits que celui d'un enfant?
La Mort savante met dans ces bières pareilles
Un symbole d'un goût bizarre et captivant,

Et lorsque j'entrevois un fantôme débile
Traversant de Paris le fourmillant tableau,
Il me semble toujours que cet être fragile
S'en va tout doucement vers un nouveau berceau;

À moins que, méditant sur la géométrie,
Je ne cherche, à l'aspect de ces membres discords,
Combien de fois il faut que l'ouvrier varie
La forme de la boîte où l'on met tous ces corps.

—

— Have you noticed how many coffins of old ladies
Are nearly as small as that of a child?
Learnèd Death posits in these caskets akin
A symbol at once bizarre and beguiling,

And when I glimpse an enfeebled phantom
Traversing the swarming tableau of Paris,
It seems always as if this fragile being
Gently carries herself toward a new cradle;

Unless, meditating upon geometry,
I think only, at the sight of discordant limbs,
Of how many times the worker must vary
The form of the box where we put every corpse.

Addressing us directly, the speaker poses the central question of the poem: —*Avez-vous observé*? But even if one *has* noticed that the coffins of little old ladies are often as small as those of children, what is the significance of this "bizarre and beguiling" symbol? What is it a symbol *of*? We are proximate to the riddle of the sphinx, to which Baudelaire alludes in "The Seven Old Men." There it was "man," here it is "woman" that is at issue. There it was unity across three phases of life that was queried; here it is the unity of birth and death. The coffin is a new cradle; an old woman traversing the swarming city gently carries herself toward it. She is thus her own mother. She gives birth to herself, and she puts herself to rest. It must be the *community* of women that is the secret of this symbol, rather than the *identity* of man. The woman who gives birth is also the woman who is born. The old men are separated into identical copies, whereas the old woman carries *herself* toward the cradle, unseparated from the one she carries. Paradoxically, the woman who is one is multiple; the man who is multiple is one. Community is expressed as the cradling of oneself as another. Identity is expressed as homogenous self-division. The debilitated corporeality of the little old ladies, which makes each one different, is what they have in common. Since the singular discordance of their limbs makes their passage laborious, such that they seem to carry themselves, they grow young as they age. The symbol recalls the great final strophe of "The Balcony," with its "suns growing young as they mount the heavens" ("Comme montent au ciel les soleil rajeunis.")[121]

But again the discourse of the speaker shifts. It seems to the speaker *as if* phantasmic old ladies gently carry themselves toward new cradles, *unless* he is caught up in technical and pragmatic considerations: how many different shapes of coffins must the worker construct for differently discordant bodies? Which is the adequate symbol: the *different* form of the box for different old women, or the *same* form of the box for old

[121] FE, 144-147.

women and children? But the question answers itself through its articulation in the *poem*: the poem is that mysteriously mutable container which is formally regular yet able to accommodate content of radically different scales, from the gardens of Tivoli, or the powerful Hippogriff, to the child that makes of her mother a transpierced Madonna. It can even construct a perfectly determinate place to hold an unmentioned honeybee, or for an unspoken name known only to the buried prompter. Indeed, the poem is the prompter's coffin—in its silences, within all the room it makes for what it doesn't say, the forgotten names of the dead are right on the tip of the tongue. The geometry of the poem writes the properties of the unconscious like the diagonal of a unit square writes the value of the square root of 2: the form is determined; the expansion is indefinite.

Like the geometrical representation of that irrational number, the actual is mystery incarnate. Thus its ground is not the determination of every one of its discordant members, but the capacity to form a particular expression—to constitute the determinacy of the finite amid the dispersion of the infinite, without surrendering its relation to the latter. Such are the fruits of pondering geometry and of contemplating poetry. They both involve the *making* of what they think, the strange concreteness of pure intuitions, the forever unspoken honeybee held in the mind's eye. Amid the forgetting of what was once venerated, amid the estranging destinies and denigrations of the social field, the poet situates himself in the poem as the one who follows and who sees, who submits to blind obedience and who surveils from afar, who is transformed by protective affection into another parental figure:

> Mais moi, moi qui de loin tendrement vous surveille,
> L'oeil inquiet, fixé sur vos pas incertains,
> Tout comme si j'étais votre père, ô merveille!
> Je goûte à votre insu des plaisirs clandestins:

Je vois s'épanouir vos passions novices;
Sombres ou lumineux, je vis vos jours perdus;
Mon coeur multiplié jouit de tous vos vices!
Mon âme resplendit de toutes vos vertus!

Ruines! ma famille! ô cerveaux congénères!
Je vous fais chaque soir un solennel adieu!
Où serez-vous demain, Eves octogénaires,
Sur qui pèse la griffe effroyable de Dieu?

—

But I, I who tenderly surveil you from afar,
Restless eye, fixed upon your uncertain steps,
As though I were your father, o marvel!
Unknown to you I taste clandestine pleasures:

I see the flowering of your novice passions;
Somber or luminous, I live your lost days;
My multiplied heart enjoys all your vices!
My soul is resplendent with all your virtues!

Ruins! my family! o congenerous brains!
I bid you each evening a solemn adieu!
Where will you be tomorrow, octogenarian Eves,
Upon whom presses God's fearsome claw?

The import of the paternal metaphor, the marvel it inscribes, is that the speaker becomes at once younger and older than the old women. Insofar as he takes them as family, he is divided from self-identity, such that he becomes both parent and child, participating in the riddle of the old sphinx as well as in the riddle of the new cradle. He does not fall into the hostile iterative solitude of "The Seven Old Men" because he is *riddled* by affection. He does not become or observe an inexorable copy, but rather becomes at once determinate and unknown, just as his restless eye is fixed upon uncertain steps. His heart is multiplied and his soul is resplendent, such that his subjective identity is both divided by and suffused with identification. The sinuous folds of old capitals have become the sinuous folds of congenerous brains, a splendidly corporeal metaphor that materializes the social thinking of the poem. In "Les Deux Bonnes Soeurs," the poet is characterized as "the enemy of the family,"[122] but here *ruins* become a family the poet can be part of. The ruin of the classical—the modern—becomes the family of ruins: des vieilles capitales, les petites vieilles.

The final lines emblazon the poem's significance as a rebus encoding the narrative puzzles of poetic determination, precisely by querying the indeterminacy of story: what happens next? To be pressed by God's fearsome claw is be determined by mortality, pinned down to earth by the powerful Hippogriff we had asked to carry us to heaven, or by the cat that strolls in Baudelaire's brain. Yet "Where will you be tomorrow?" is a question of indetermination, of contingency, of the unknown future. To determine to be determined, voluntarily surrendering autonomy to sociality, is to mediate determination and indetermination. That mediation is the essence of the actual. To hold it together in the element of the particular is the work of the poem, and here it sustains the idea *as* the particular: not just God, but God's *fearsome claw*. The *way* the poem holds particulars together is articulated through infinitely subtle determinations (we cannot foreclose their number), but that articulation is also compressed into a single question, addressed to a singular figure of the plurality of being: to "octogenarian Eves." Turning the most well-worn cliché into something that had never been said before—into a daily and yet unprecedented question—is as intimate to the frail being of poetry as the existence of an unmentioned honeybee, as the embroidery of a purse clutched at the hip. The fatal humor of the question is transpierced by light comedy through an estranging signifier—*octogénaire*—out

[122] FE, 394-395.

of place among the mythic and religious, and that estrangement makes the universality of the question particular. Meanwhile, the archetypal gravity of the question makes the particular universal: the elderly daughters of modernity become the first mothers of a mythic past, growing young as they carry themselves to a new cradle. Poetry teaches us how to participate in the congenerous without turning correspondences into credo, and thus how to look without loathing upon contradiction, how to cradle it in our arms while observing it from afar, how to taste its clandestine pleasures with complicit innocence. Let us love it, for contradiction is the broken body of the soul itself, its multiplied heart: the concrete being of spirit. Thus poetry—not philosophy or science or theology—is its discourse.

The Existence of the Poem

Among Émile Benveniste's fascinating notes for an unwritten study of Baudelaire, one finds a page on which a single word is written: *abîme*. [Figure 6] The archival and editorial processes have appended their contributions: BnF stamp overlapping the underlined word; Chloé Laplantine's transcription from script to type on the facing page; numbering of folder, sheet, and archival order; description of paper, dimensions, writing implement, ink color (blue in the original). Ghosts of the words on the back of the leaves pass through to the hither side. At the top of the pages, we find the pagination of the edited volume itself, alongside the author's name on the left and his subject's name on the right—which raises a question about the author function. Is the word written on the recto Baudelaire's or Benveniste's? Is the word printed on the verso Benveniste's or Laplantine's? It is so difficult for a word to remain alone on a page. As soon as it attracts attention, its scriptural solitude is imperiled. The abyss is restless. Shouldn't something be added?

The dialectical elegance of Benveniste's notation is that its inscription cancels what it designates: the abyss of the blank page. The note is like a lovely predecessor of Mallarmé drawn from Baudelaire, retroactively suspended between them. Given the appearance of the word *abîme* upon the empty expanse of "cette blancheur rigide,"[123] one could only expect further inscriptions to follow, a dialectical proliferation of stamped signs and structural determinations setting the signifier not only in a certain position with respect to other signifiers, printed on other pages, but also with respect to institutional codes and

---

123 Stéphane Mallarmé, *Un coup de des n'abolira le hasard* (Paris: Gallimard, 1914), unpaginated.

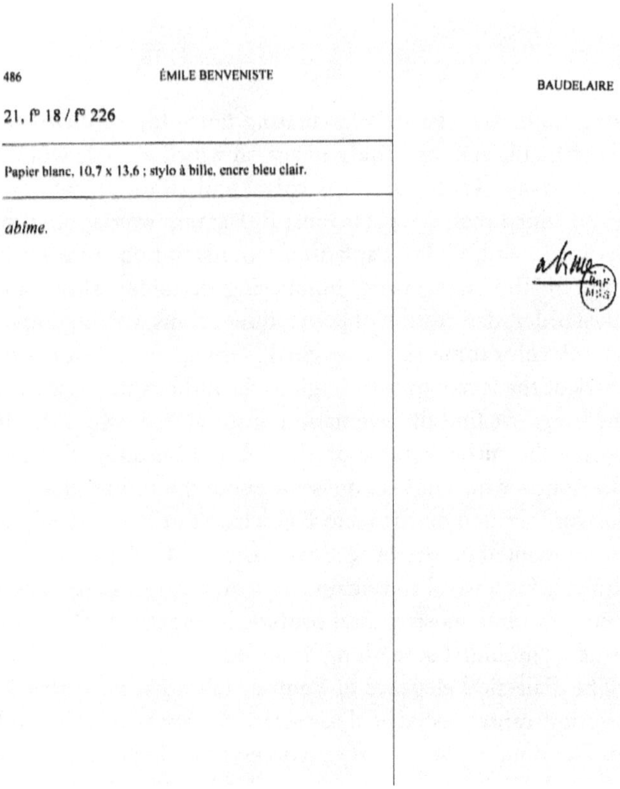

486 ÉMILE BENVENISTE	BAUDELAIRE
21, f° 18 / f° 226	
Papier blanc, 10,7 x 13,6 ; stylo à bille, encre bleu clair.	
abîme.	

FIGURE 6: Emile Benveniste, *Baudelaire*, Edited and Transcribed by Chloé Laplantine

scholarly protocols of reception. A word *in* Baudelaire drawn *from* Baudelaire and inscribed upon a fresh page is no longer a word in Baudelaire. But perhaps it both is and is not, since, for the reader of Les Fleurs du Mal, Benveniste's inscription will resonate with the traces of Baudelaire's usages, with the remembrance of their contexts, with the relations among poems in which the word was deployed, with the proximity of its sense to that of other words, like *gouffre* or *vide* or *néant*. So the word remains "chez Baudelaire" even when drawn outside the world of his poems, since its context in the notes sustains traces of their determinations, which now—strange force of inscription—hover above the blank. It is in fact the only page of Benveniste's notes, among three hundred and sixty-one sheets, on which a word appears alone.

On the following sheet there is a brief list of words for sounds:

sons

retentir (très expressif)
échos
son(s) sonore
chant, chanson
mélodieux (1 fois)

On the previous sheet we find:

Grands principes
âme ange(s) (-élique / inconnu)
esprit

On nearby pages there is a list titled "rares"—ami, s'amuser, s'anéantir—or just the words "art, *art*, artiste." But *abîme* claims the privilege of a page unto itself (before it enters the archive), as if to free it of all context, to give it a world of its own. And even having surrendered its solitude it looks at home there. The imprimatur of the BnF somehow suits it—a boulder on which to lean—as does its relation to the typeset word "Baudelaire," below which it drifts like the name's true signature. The page number, 487, will do well enough: the first digit doubles itself into the second, as if 4 had initially stemmed from 0, while the last is drawn from the second by subtraction (- 1). One must imagine *abîme* happy.

"Just a word on the page and there is the drama,"[124] writes Sarah Kane. She does so while writing a play, though one whose script is at the limit of dramatic form, where it intersects with poetry precisely through its use of the page as a visual field. Just a word on the page and there is the poem? Benveniste's inscription begs the elementary question of what a word means, and of how the meaning of words is altered by poetic language—which is precisely the problem he is grappling with in his notes on Baudelaire. The sequence of sheets with lists of words in which *abîme* appears, running for about thirty pages in folder 21, seems to be initiated by a passage from A.N. Whitehead's *Symbolism*, typed out under the heading "Symbols and words in poetry":

> Why do we say that the word "tree", spoken or written, is a symbol to us for trees? Both the word itself and trees themselves enter into our experience on equal terms; and it would be just as sensible, viewing the matter abstractly, for trees to symbolize the word "tree" as for the word to symbolize the trees.
>
> This is certainly true and humane [sic.] nature sometimes works that way. For example, if you are a poet and wish to write a lyric on trees, you will walk into the forest in order that the trees may suggest the appropriate words. Thus for the poet in his ecstasy—or perhaps agony—of composition the trees are the symbols and the words are

---

124 Sarah Kane, 4.48 *Psychosis* in *Complete Plays* (London: Methuen, 2001), 213.

the meaning. He concentrates on the trees in order to get at the words.

...The poet is a person for whom visual sights and sounds and emotional experiences refer symbolically to words. The poet's readers are people for whom his words refer symbolically to the visual sights and sounds and emotions he wants to evoke.[125]

Setting aside the heuristic example, the point is that, for Whitehead, the poet is one for whom the tree is the symbol and the word the meaning (sights, sounds, and emotions refer symbolically to words), while the poet's readers will reverse the order of determination—from word back to sight, sound, or emotion. But how exactly does *the poem*, between inscription and reading, mediate these two orders of reference?

Benveniste, apparently both before and after his transcription of the passage from Whitehead, works toward a similar approach to the motivation and reference of poetic signs.[126] He writes that "the sentiment which moves the poet, the experience which makes his sensibility vibrate and engenders within him an emotional state, is that which he tries to translate in words. He chooses, he conjoins words to reproduce this emotion."[127] The poet is the one who draws words from emotions, from vibrations of sensibility. Benveniste holds that in "ordinary language" the referent is *exterior* to the sign, in the world (even if the referent is purely noetic), while in "poetic language" the referent is *interior* to the expression enunciated: "here the signifieds are subordinated to the emotional intention, they thus restore the intended emotion by themselves being words of a certain phonetic form (length, sound) and of a certain construction (order,

---

125 A.N. Whitehead quoted in Benveniste, *Baudelaire*, 463.
126 For a superb discussion of Benveniste's treatment of poetic language in his notes on Baudelaire, see Chloé Laplantine, *Émile Benveniste, l'inconscient et le poème* (Limoges: Éditions Lambert-Lucas, 2011).
127 Benveniste, *Baudelaire*, 28-29.

conjunction, coupling, repetition)."[128] The *form* and *construction* of the words—the relation of their qualities and quantities, the order into which they are composed—is what renders the emotion. The formal construction of the words returns *us* to *it*: to the feeling, the desire, the sensation, the vibration that traverses the poet. Thus "the reference of ordinary language is of an objective-conceptual nature. The reference of poetry is subjective-emotional."[129]

For Benveniste, the priority of the expressive, of subjective-emotional reference, is not at odds with the determination of meaning by form. He finds "a fundamental principle of poetic language" in the submission of language "to the *form* (or the structure) of verse, of rhyme, of the strophe, which is the structure of the *poem*."[130] For example, he refers to the set of possibilities for rhyme attending each word as a *paradigme poématique* and to the relation of measure to the selection of words as a *syntagmatique poématique*.[131] For the translator of poetry, these "poematic" dimensions of its language are set in stark relief: if a word at the end of a line is partially determined by the necessity of rhyme, does that determination become contingent when the rhyme is lost in translation? Could one exchange it for a synonymous word if the latter is better suited to the rhythmic demands of the translation? For example, given the close proximity of *abîme* and *gouffre* in the lexicon of Baudelaire's poems, their possible interchangeability for the purpose of rhyme, is it permissible to use "abyss" and "gulf" interchangeably when translating to English? Obviously it depends, but rhyme and meter make one attentive to the manner in which the *selection* of words among possible alternatives puts them in relation to those which go *unselected*, such that the unwritten and unsaid

---

128 Benveniste, *Baudelaire*, 28-29.
129 Benveniste, *Baudelaire*, 298-399.
130 Benveniste, *Baudelaire*, 662-663.
131 Benveniste, *Baudelaire*, 662-663.

tremble on the cusp of poetic articulation. Hence the value of making lists of closely related words while studying a poet. Determinations of poetic language (relations between selected/unselected) lend priority to sound and rhythm in ways that profoundly affect meaning. Words become charged not only with their own meaning, and the relational meanings of rhyme, but also with the meaning *of their selection*—of their relation to a virtual reservoir of words that do not enter the poem yet are also somehow within it. "Prunelle" may be used rather than "oeil" according to the demands of rhyme or meter, but it may be unclear whether the specificity of the former is motivated by meaning or sound. There is always a sense in which words are metonyms of their own meaning; poetry activates and illuminates that sense in curious ways.

When Benveniste writes that "the poetic composition determines, to a certain extent, the poetic language," he means this in the radical sense that what we encounter in poetry is *not the same language* as that of the dictionary, though it consists of the same words. He poses the question with simple clarity:

> It is quite certain that the linguistic material which the poet uses is that of the dictionary. Save for rare exceptions, all the words of Baudelaire, of Mallarmé, are individually in the dictionary. There is no new verbal form, the rection of the prepositions is the same, etc. And yet it is not the same language. Why?[132]

It is not that poetic language breaks altogether with the referential dimension of ordinary language, but that reference undergoes *incalculable* deviations from its general sense. Transmutations of "the dictionary" by poetic language belong to "emotion" and they also belong to "form," to the relation between these: the formally determined relation of signifiers is essential to creating an "interior" emotional sense rather than an "exterior" referential

132 Benveniste, *Baudelaire*, 444-445.

meaning. The poem, or the volume of poems (in the case of *Les Fleurs du Mal*), creates a world which is not distinct from the world in which it participates but is rather a modulation of its conceptual parameters, of the world's relation to language, such that one has to learn anew the subtle cues that shape the sense of signs amongst themselves.

For example, we could produce a partial survey of the poetic world we explored in the previous chapter through a mere list of grouped words:

vide, abîme	ténèbres, ombre	rhythme, parfum
gouffre, mêler	enivrer, inonder	lueur, sinueux
confonder	oublier	fourmiller, fertile

cité, cerveau, ruine, famille, âme, corps, coeur

Here the relation between *lueur* and *cerveau* would depend not on the definitions of the words but upon our understanding of how minimal sensory qualities differentiated from shadow or void may merge into tempting metaphysical correspondences, blend into the intoxication of an erotic swoon, or flicker through sinuous city streets among strangers, mediating the familial recognition of congenerous brains or marking the bitter eyes of a hostile and inexorable copy.

Or consider the opening quatrain of Baudelaire's great sonnet, "Obsession":

Grand bois, vous m'effrayez comme des cathédrales;
Vous hurlez comme l'orgue; et dans nos coeurs maudits,
Chambres d'éternal deuil où vibrent de vieux râles,
Répondent les échos de vos *De profundis*.

—

> Deep woods, you frighten me like cathedrals;
> You howl like the organ; and in our damned hearts,
> Chambers of eternal mourning where old death rattles vibrate,
> Respond the echoes of your *De profundis*.[133]

One might almost *see* "l'orage" in "l'orgue," as the woods howl like the organ. The old death rattles still vibrating within damned hearts will be those of the wounded soldier in "La Cloche Fêlée." The chambers of eternal mourning will be those occupied by the love at last sight of "À Une Passante," where the fugitive beauty of a women "en grand deuil" led the speaker to ask "Ne te verrai-je plus que dans l'éternité?" ("Shall I see you no more till eternity?"). What is it that motivates the analogy constructed in this quatrain, which turns woods into cathedrals through the fear they inspire? The meaning of the analogy is the *emotion* it communicates, which is a complex form of fear. It involves the dread of damnation, the sorrow of mourning, the corporeality of death, the eeriness of prayer. And it seems to involve the *hollowness* of the exterior experienced as an interior, of the cavity of the chest one hears in hymns or in respiration, the relation between the throat and the pipes of an organ, the uncanniness of *having a body* when one is supposed to *be a soul*. To rhyme *cathédrales* with *râles* is to inscribe a shaking of foundations proximate to the last line of Gautier's *Ténèbres*: "Le Dieu ne viendra pas. L'Église est renversée." ("God will not come. The Church is overthrown."). It is the fear of the speaker that folds exteriority into interiority, expanding the *emptiness* of the latter, and this communicates the shaking of his subjective foundations, the last gasp that barely escapes the body as it succumbs to being only itself. It is something like the fear of the *abyss*, the *De profundis* that echoes in the hollow heart within the hollow chest, and that makes an empty object of the void. If one wanted to know what *abîme* means in Baudelaire, this

---

133 FE, 262-263.

would be a good quatrain to consider, though the word does not appear therein.[134]

This is not to position the word *abîme* as a hypogram that is embedded within or that generates this quatrain of "Obsession." Rather, it is to note that the meaning of words, in a literary work, may not be bound to the context of their appearance, while the sense of a passage may not reside in relations among the words it includes. There is an *absence* that haunts the literary production of meaning which is not necessarily that of *something else*, an absent word, but rather of the *separation* of sense from the exteriority of reference. In *Toward a Theory of Literary Production*, Pierre Macherey puts forward a theory of the literary work that will help us think through the complex relation between negativity and determinacy upon which the existence of poetic language depends. The literary work, Macherey argues, "exists above all through its determinate absences, through what it does not say, through its relation to what it is not."[135] Yet he also argues that "the work is determined: it is itself, and nothing other. The moment this is understood, it becomes the object of a rational study."[136] We are to understand the literary work as determined insofar as it is nothing other than itself, yet also as constituted by its determinate absences, by its relation to what it is not. It is the *existence* of the literary work that is specified by this double criterion.

---

134 Paul de Man notes "the recurrent image of the subject's presence to itself as a spatial enclosure, room, tomb, or crypt in which the voice echoes as in a cave. The image draws it verisimilitude from its own "mise en abyme" in the shape of the body as the *container* of the voice (or soul, heart, breath, consciousness, spirit, etc.) that it exhales." "Anthropomorphism and Trope in the Lyric" in *The Rhetoric of Romanticism* (New York: Columbia University Press, 1984), 256.

135 Pierre Macherey, *Pour une théorie de la production littéraire* (Paris: ENS Éditions, 2014), 148. All translations from this edition are my own.

136 Macherey, *Pour une théorie de la production littéraire*, 46.

Like Benveniste, Macherey is concerned with the transmutation of ordinary language by its literary usage, with the strange fact that it both is and is not the "same" language:

> The novelty of this language consists in the fact that its only meaning is that which it gives itself: having nothing, apparently, behind it or before it, not being haunted by any foreign presence, this language is autonomous insofar as it is effectively without depth, its surface entirely unfolded. Thus, in order to distinguish itself from ordinary language, it fundamentally has no need to coin new words: weaving them into the relations of a text, words are made into something other than words, and, once torn from their ordinary connections and inaugurated into a different order, a new "reality" emerges. We will say again that this transmutation consists entirely in the production of a tautology.[137]

Words are *woven* into textual relations. What is thus constituted is a *surface* without depth. Words become *something other* than words. The new reality thus produced consists in the *production of a tautology*. The literary work *is itself and nothing other* insofar as its reality is not of the same order as that from which its words are drawn. The weaving of words into a literary work is the negation of the given and the production of the made. The tautological character of the work consists in the determinate surface, "entirely unfolded," that emerges from the negativity of this making. The work is not what it is not because it is what it is.

To this strange tautology, designating the plane of the work's existence, corresponds an equally strange contradiction in the activity of critical reading. According to Macherey, "the work must be elaborated, *treated*, or else it will never be a theoretical fact, an object of knowledge; but it must also be *left* as it is, or else one will bring to bear upon it a value judgment

---

137 Macherey, *Pour une théorie de la production littéraire*, 50.

and not a theoretical judgment."[138] We must elaborate the work while leaving it as it is. We are not to recover or reconstitute a latent meaning; rather we must constitute a *new* knowledge, which is appended to the text we read.[139] The work does not mean *one thing* which could be discovered, for "the necessity of the work is founded upon the multiplicity of its meanings."[140] That multiplicity is a function of what the work *does not say* as much as what it says, such that we are to understand what is lacking in a text, which makes it nothing other than what it is, rather than discovering the latent meaning of what the text says, into which it could be translated. "What the work does not say, it *manifests*, it lays bare, in its very letter: it is made of nothing other. This silence gives it its existence."[141] It is this silence that must be treated without cancelling it, such that we elaborate the work while leaving it as it is. In a crucial formulation, Macherey states that "rather than that of *structure*, the essential concept of such analysis will be that of *dislocation (décalage)*."[142] In order to respect the specificity of literary production, the critic is to grasp its dislocation from the givenness of language by performing a dislocation of literary interpretation: we explore the peculiar reticence of poetic language by studying its displacements of meaning, the negativity of its consistency, the absences inhering in its woven surface. But we will see how such a critical method may also be consonant with Benveniste's emphasis upon the rendering of emotion by poetic language.

Let us now return to "Obsession" in order to study the manner in which it articulates, divides, and dislocates a major figural locus in *Les Fleurs du Mal* and in nineteenth century French poetry more broadly. We will show how, in the final tercet of that sonnet, the function of metaphor not only separates

---

138 Macherey, *Pour une théorie de la production littéraire*, 79.
139 Macherey, *Pour une théorie de la production littéraire*, 16.
140 Macherey, *Pour une théorie de la production littéraire*, 79.
141 Macherey, *Pour une théorie de la production littéraire*, 84.
142 Macherey, *Pour une théorie de la production littéraire*, 150.

poetic language from ordinary language, but also counters the operation of metaphor itself, suspending its movement so as to open a distance or gap, a rift (*écart*) internal to its figural logic. This suspension is enabled by what is not said through a single word, by the displacements of significance it manifests and that it thus renders finite, determinate. Elaborating this suspension will allow us not to exchange the poem for an interpretation, but to display the tautology of its existence, which is its splendor.

* * *

As it moves through the quatrains and tercets of the sonnet form, "Obsession" weaves together grammatical alterations and displacements of subject and object that are signaled by internal rhyme. Here are the opening phrases of each strophe:

> Grand bois, vous *m'efrrayez*...
> Je *te hais*, Océan!
> Comme tu *me plairais*, ô nuit!
> *Mais* les ténèbres...

The speaker is the grammatical object frightened *by* the woods. The "I" is the grammatical subject who hates the Ocean. And then, the night is the grammatical subject that *would* please the speaker, but the action of the verb upon its object is here suspended by the conditional. The speaker would be pleased by the night, "sans ces étoiles," but he is not because the stars are still there, insistent, their points of light speaking "un langage connu." It is the relation between subject (*nuit*) and object (*me*) that is suspended by the conditional, and it is suspended by a desire that, subtending the grammar of the sentence, reverses that relation. The speaker is the subject of a desire that negates the pleasure of the starry night: "Car je cherche le vide, et le noir, et le nu!" It is the *given* (the starry night sky) that is displaced by the conditional, by the desire to go beyond the objecthood of the subject, to go beyond relationality per se, to traverse the limits of grammar by breaking through the alternations of subject and object to which grammar is prone.

But, the final tercet begins with an apparent concession to the inaccessibility of the absolute. *Mais* rhymes with the verbs that have driven the opening of the previous strophes, but now the subject/object form of the poetic speaker disappears from the first line, giving way to a relation of metaphorical identity between "ténèbres" and "des toiles" before reappearing, in the second line, through a complex reciprocity of objecthood and action. Here is the full tercet:

> Mais les ténèbres sont elles-mêmes des toiles
> Où vivent, jaillaissant de mon oeil par milliers,
> Des êtres disparus aux regard familiers.
>
> —
>
> But the shadows are themselves [   ]
> Where live, bursting from my eye by thousands,
> Those vanished beings with familiar gazes.

We leave "des toiles" untranslated, because the indeterminacy of its reference will be the problem of poetic determination we intend to pursue. But note how, in the second and third lines, "des êtres disparus" become the plural grammatical subjects which *burst from* the grammatical object-form of the poetic speaker: "jaillaissant de mon oeil par milliers." The vanished beings *live* on or in "des toiles," yet they burst from "my eye," which also registers their "familiar gazes." Having been displaced from its opening line, the speaker returns to the tercet through the agency of his object, "mon oeil," which seems to both produce and receive the thousands of gazes it sees, at once the source and the sightline of those who have vanished, yet appear, who live, though they may have died: "Des êtres disparus."

M'effrayez, te hais, me plairais, mais—we are led by rhyme through the entanglements of grammar into an insistently strict identity of "ténèbres" and "des toiles"—*sont elles-mêmes*. And this identity arrives through the indirection of a qualification, which surrenders the absolute: *mais*. Now, how are we to read this strange rhetorical figure, this metaphor which is given as the remainder of an unfulfilled desire for absolute negation? What exactly *are* "les ténèbres" said to be? Again, we register the complex sense of this term—phenomenal, epistemological, spiritual, religious—that we discussed in the previous chapter. Here *les ténèbres* "are themselves" something else—*des toiles*—and we will try to situate this noun within the sense of the final tercet and within the sense of the poem, to draw out the multiplicity of its meanings without cancelling those, yet without settling into the comfort of pure indetermination—since the word *is* determinate, and there are many things it *does not* mean. The word institutes a locus of selection, of determination, that has to be read and delimited, grasped as what it is through the relation between what it is not and what it may be. We will try to hear the silence it articulates through what it says, and to see in its inscription the existence of the poem, made manifest: the stubborn tautology of its facticity, restored to the reticence of its being-there.

"Toiles" means canvases, does it not? It refers metonymically to paintings, and Baudelaire uses the word many times in just this way. In "Une Charogne" he refers to

> Une ébauche lente à venir
> Sur la toile oubliée, et que l'artiste achève
> Seulement par le souvenir.[143]

---

143 FE, 126-129.

> A sketch slow to come,
> Upon the forgotten canvas, which the artist completes
> By memory alone.

In "A Martyr," in the context of a describing "A sketch by an unknown Master," he evokes

> Un sang rouge et vivant, dont la toile s'abreuve
> Avec l'avidité d'un pré.
>
> —
>
> A vivid red blood, which the canvas drinks
> With the avidity of a meadow.[144]

In both cases, the context clearly determines "la toile" as the canvas of a painting, forgotten or viscerally present. In his notes to "Obsession" in the *Oeuvres Complètes*, Claude Pichois points to the first section of "A Phantom," where the speaker laments:

> Je suis comme un peintre qu'un Dieu moqueur
> Condamne à peindre, hélas! sur les ténèbres;
>
> —
>
> I am like a painter whom a mocking God
> Condemns to paint, alas! upon shadows;[145]

Here we have a figure of the shadow-canvas as the medium of creative futility, a dark obscurity by which a mocking God condemns artistic production to failure.[146] Pichois also points to a passage in *Artificial Paradises* where Baudelaire describes

---

144 FE, 370-375.
145 FE, 150-155.
146 Indeed, Baudelaire sent "Une fantôme" and "Obsession" to Poulet-Malassis together. On March 13, 1860 he writes to inquire, "have you received 'Obsession' and 'Un fantôme'?"

"la singulière faculté d'apercevoir, ou plutôt de créer, sur la toile féconde des ténèbres tout un monde de visions bizarres" ("the singular faculty of perceiving, or rather of creating, upon the fecund canvas of shadows a whole world of bizarre visions").[147] Here the shadow-canvas is a figure of imaginative fecundity, rather than artistic damnation, and this may seem more closely aligned with the "toiles" of "Obsession," upon which the gazes of vanished beings live, "bursting from my eye by thousands." Crucially, Baudelaire also deploys the term in order to analogize painting and writing in a discussion of compositional method:

> il faut donc se hâter lentement...pour écrire vite, il faut avoir beaucoup pensé, — avoir trimballé un sujet avec soi, à la promenade, au bain, au restaurant, et presque chez sa maîtresse...La toile doit être couverte—en esprit—au moment où l'écrivain prend la plume pour écrire le titre.
>
> —
>
> One must hurry slowly...to write quickly, one must have thought a great deal, — have lugged a subject around with oneself, to the promenade, to the bath, to the restaurant, and nearly to one's mistress...The canvas must be covered—in the mind—at the moment when the writer takes the pen to write the title.[148]

The page is the canvas that must already be covered, by reflection, even as one begins to write. At the limit of this image we find the *absolutely* covered canvas, the monochrome: the poem that would correspond to the starless sky would be an already blacked out page. But *les ténèbres* are a concession to mediation, to the stars that are already there, to a darkness that is not absolute, to the shadows deriving from the relation of light to opacity. If the shadows are themselves canvases, then we are in the world of mediation, of *particular* figures and signifiers.

---

147 Pichois in Baudelaire, Oeuvres Complètes I, 480.
148 Baudelaire, *Conseils aux jeune littérateurs* in Oeuvres Complètes I, 17.

But "toiles" can also mean "webs," and we find the plural noun used in this sense in "Sépultre," just eight poems prior to "Obsession." There a burial is imagined on a "dark and heavy night" ("une nuit lourde et sombre"),

À l'heure où les chastes étoiles
Ferment leurs yeux appesantis,
L'araignée y fera ses toiles,
Et la vipère ses petits;

—

At the hour when the chaste stars
Close their heavy eyes,
There shall the spider make her webs,
And the viper her brood;[149]

As in "Obsession," *toiles* is rhymed with *étoiles*, and the spider's web would seem to provide an apt figure of concession to the persistence of those stars that are wished away in the previous tercet, shining through the darkness like points in a network of invisible filaments. Thus we would have a network of filaments woven by an arachnid, rather than a human being, upon which living prey, rather than artistic compositions, are captured. In this case, the mesh of the textile is both a home on which beings live and a trap in which they die. We can see how these connotations of the web may be figuratively associated with the fabric of artistic representation, as in Maya Deren's *Meshes of the Afternoon* or the funeral shroud Penelope weaves and unravels, detaining the suitors and linking death, mourning, and capture with the duplicity of artistic making and unmaking. One might then seek a synthetic meaning of the metaphor determining "ténèbres" as "des toiles": a symbol combining the artist/spider as figure of a constructive yet obscure making (*poiesis*), at once domestic and uncanny, dangerous and sustaining, natural and

[149] FE, 244-245.

surreal, intentional and unconscious—as in Joanne Kyger's *The Tapestry and the Web*:

> and what am I?
> a flower
> a deer
> a spider waiting
> > for the breeze to
> > speed my weaving
>
> > the reverie of
>
> > memory past
> > what I know.[150]

The role Kyger attributes to her lyric speaker—a spider waiting as it weaves the reverie of memory—is attributed by Deleuze to the narrator of Proust's *Récherche*:

> The Search is not constructed like a cathedral or like a gown, but like a web. The spider-Narrator, whose web is the Search being spun, being woven by each thread stirred by one sign or another: the web and the spider, the web and the body are one and the same machine.[151]

This hybrid figure of the canvas-web would also be a figure of the page-poem, and the weaving of signs would be accompanied by the woven fabric of the double figure itself, complex yet coherent, intertwining painter, spider, and poet within the shadowy textures of metaphor.

---

150 Joanne Kyger, *The Tapestry and the Web* (San Francisco: Four Seasons Foundation, 1965), 19.

151 Gilles Deleuze, *Proust and Signs*, trans. Richard Howard (Minneapolis: University of Minnesota Press, 2000), 182.

Yet this potentially satisfying interpretive synthesis is interrupted by another possibility, which is more overtly intertextual. Since we are familiar with Poe's "Shadow—A Parable," we may recognize the similarity of its final sentence to Baudelaire's tercet. Here again is that sentence in Baudelaire's translation:[152]

> Et alors, tous les sept, nous nous dressâmes d'horreur sur nos siéges, et nous nous tenions tremblants, frissonants, effarés; car le timbre de la voix de l'ombre n'était pas le timbre d'un seul individu, mais d'une multitude d'êtres; et cette voix, variant ses inflexions de syllable en syllable, tombait confusément dans nos oreilles en imitant les accents connus et familiers de mille et mille amis disparus![153]

In the tones of the shadow's voice evoked by Poe, rendered as "les accents connus et familiers de mille et milles amis disparus," we recognize Baudelaire's "êtres disparus aux regards familiers," which are described as "jaillissant de mon oeil par milliers." Baudelaire has performed a sensory transposition of the voice of Poe's shadow, from sound to vision, as the familiar gazes of disappeared beings now burst from the eye rather than falling confusedly into the ears. If we recall that the Shadow which speaks at the end of Poe's tale has stepped forward from among sable draperies, we may note that *toiles* can refer metonymically to curtains—as it does at the end of "Le Rêve d'un Curieux":

> J'étais comme l'enfant avide du spectacle,
> Haïssant le rideau comme on hait un obstacle...
> Enfin la verité froide se révéla:

---

152 The link is suggested by Crépet in his notes to Baudelaire's translation of the tale, as well as by Pichois in his notes to "Obsession." See M. Jacques Crépet, ed., *Oeuvres Complètes de Charles Baudelaire, Nouvelles Historie Extraordinaires* (Paris: Libraire-Éditeur, 1917), 493 and Baudelaire, *Oeuvres Complètes* I, 981.

153 Baudelaire, trans., "Ombre" in *Nouvelles Histoires Extraordinaires*, 493.

J'étais mort sans surprise, et la terrible aurore
M'enveloppait. —Eh quoi! n'est-ce donc que cela?
La toile était levée et j'attendais encore.

—

I was like the child avid for the spectacle,
Hating the curtain as one hates an obstacle...
At last the cold truth was revealed:

I was uneventfully dead, and the terrible dawn
Enveloped me. —What! is that it?
The curtain had risen and I was still waiting.[154]

In this poem Baudelaire can refer first to *le rideau* and then to *la toile* to designate the same object; thus he might similarly transform *les draperies*, from his translation of Poe, into *des toiles* according to the demands of rhyme, while substituting *les ténèbres* for *l'ombres* according to the demands of meter. Poetic form would then play a crucial role in understanding not only why the poem says what it says (*des toiles* rhymes with *étoiles*), but also how *what it does not say* makes it what it is. It does not say *les rideaus*, or *les draperies*, but the silence of these words issues in the sound of a word suited to the demands of rhyme and meter. If we read "des toiles" as the curtains wherein Poe's Shadow lives, then at the end of both tale and poem we have the advent of the living dead, of their familiar gazes and their well-known accents, at once startling and strangely intimate. And in each case it would be a multitude at issue, stemming from the grammatical renunciation of the starless sky or the tone of a single voice: "*Mais* les ténèbres;" "car le timbre de la voix de l'ombre n'était pas le timbre d'un seul individu, *mais d'une multitude d'êtres*."

An intertextual reading through Poe's tale is justified and illuminating. It makes sense of the strange and complex image

---

154 FE, 440-441.

in the tercet: the shadows live in the curtains, and the apparition of the dead within them bursts from my own eyes. Thus we see the stakes of how we interpret the referent of *des toiles*. If we understand it as canvases or webs, the intertextual reference no longer coheres. If we understand it as curtains, the image of the artist-spider or the canvas-page falls away. Yet we have to grant that each of these readings is feasible, that they interfere with one another, and thus that the *world* of Poe's story, which might otherwise fuse with the world of Baudelaire's poem, is at least partially displaced. Intertextual reference, precisely by virtue of being intertextual, is disrupted by the non-referential world of the poem. We could say that the poem draws Poe's tale into itself, but it doesn't let it back out. We can include Poe's shadow in Baudelaire's shadows, in the darkness of his poem, and thus we can weave it into Baudelaire's web, but Poe's draperies will then be woven into the fabric of the poem, such that his tale will no longer be what it was before. Suddenly the room in the tale will appear as a painting, the disappeared friends with whom it concludes will be so many insects caught in a web.

Thus we recognize the *determinacy* of the poem. It says "toiles." That does not have to *mean* curtains, or canvases, or webs. Yet it does draw these referential senses into its semantic field. Because it does not say "l'araignée," like "Sepulcher," it can be taken to refer to Poe's curtains. Because it does not say "draperies," like Poe's "Shadow," it can be taken to refer to a web, and thus does not quite coincide with the world of Poe's tale. The poem includes by excluding, and it excludes by including. The *selection* of a word is complex, insofar as it drags the unselected with it while expelling it at the same time. At the locus of a single signifier, Baudelaire's poem generates a determinate field of indetermination, enriching the final tercet with slightly incompatible yet synthetically suggestive connotations. The glimmer of oil paint becomes the glint of a spider's eye; the fold of a curtain becomes the shade of chiaroscuro; the tautness of a web becomes the stretch of the canvas. Because our reading of "The Seven Old Men" has mingled the familiar dead of Delacroix's *The Barque of Dante* with those of Poe's parable, those rising from the river Styx may now mingle with the familiar gazes of "Obsession." Is the unquiet water from which they rise a shadowy curtain? Are a thousand tones a thousand gazes? Are the stars akin, by the grace of rhyme, to an articulated textile within which web, canvas, and curtain are one? Or must there be a multitude of beings, a true division of the metaphor, a mutual repulsion of its plausible vehicles, rather than their absorption into one figure, "le timbre d'un seul individu"? Is the voice of the shadow itself—which contains a multitude of tones—one or many? There are cathedrals—echoing with *De profundis*, shadowy amid Tenebrae—where one would find paintings, webs, and draperies together, though they would be distinct. Are we in a church or a forest of symbols? If a stanza is a room, is a word itself a room? Is a heart within a chest a chamber? How many such questions may we pose while still *making sense*? "Might we even come to 'cherish the questions themselves,' as Rilke once advised his young poet, 'like closed rooms, like books written in a very strange tongue'? Might we even begin constituting, indeed, a collection, an entire library of questions?"[155] Is a metaphor a library of questions? Is a cathedral a library of metaphors? Do the webs of spiders tremble at the howl of the organ? Are the curtains of the confessional akin to the draperies in the paintings? How many confessions may be heard in the gazes of those paintings, bursting from my eye? Metaphor, its multitudes, brings us to the brink of delirium.

Yet Macherey tells us that "the necessity of the work is founded upon the multiplicity of its meanings."[156] What does that mean, the *necessity* of the work, and how might we account for it amid the contingency of questions? We can try to grasp the stakes of this formulation by considering Paul de Man's approach

---

[155] Gustaf Sobin, *Luminous Debris: Reflecting on Vestige in Provence and Languedoc* (Berkeley: University of California Press, 1999), 54-55.

[156] Macherey, *Pour une théorie de la production littéraire*, 79.

to "Obsession" in his famous essay, "Anthropomorphism and Trope in the Lyric."[157] The essay turns around de Man's positioning of "Obsession" as Baudelaire's own *lyrical reading* of "Correspondences," which transforms its impersonal, third person discourse into the rhetoric of first person expression. According to de Man, this tranformation performs "a defensive motion of understanding,"[158] a hermeneutic reduction of figural ambiguity through the recuperation of subjective address and "the reconciliation of knowledge with phenomenal, aesthetic experience."[159] On this basis, de Man offers the rather withering judgment that "'Obsession' translates 'Correspondances' into intelligibility, the least one can hope for in a successful reading."[160] "We all perfectly and quickly understand 'Obsession,'" he writes, but this understanding "leaves 'Correspondances' as thoroughly incomprehensible as it always was."[161] For de Man, "Correspondences" resists interpretation, while "Obsession" transforms the earlier poem's mysterious tropes into a series of readily legible lyric figures.

De Man's reading of "Correspondences" is brilliantly subtle. He draws out the tension between analogy and enumeration in the poem, which disrupts the totalizing claim of metaphor—its promised "transport"—through the "stutter" of potentially endless repetition.[162] His reading of "Obsession," on the other hand, is uncharacteristically reductive. De Man *himself* performs a defensive movement of the understanding in order to assimilate the poem to ready legibility. At the core of this operation is his reading of the word "toiles." Noting the "metaphoric crossing between perception and hallucination" in the poem's final tercet, de Man argues that this

---

157 Paul de Man, "Anthropomorphism and Trope in the Lyric" in *The Rhetoric of Romanticism*, New York: Columbia University Press, 1984, 239-262.

158 de Man, "Anthropomorphism and Trope in the Lyric," 261.

159 de Man, "Anthropomorphism and Trope in the Lyric," 258.

160 de Man, "Anthropomorphism and Trope in the Lyric," 259.

161 de Man, "Anthropomorphism and Trope in the Lyric," 261.

162 de Man, "Anthropomorphism and Trope in the Lyric," 250, 259.

occurs by means of the paraphernalia of painting, which is also that of recollection and of re-cognition, as the recovery, to the senses, of what seemed to be forever beyond experience. In an earlier outline, Baudelaire had written

> Mais les ténèbres sont elles-mêmes des toiles
> Où [peint] ... (presumably for "se peignent"; O.C. , 1:981)

"Peint" confirms the reading of "toiles" as the device by means of which painters or dramatists project the space or the stage of representation, by enframing the interiorized expanse of the skies.[163]

De Man has recourse to a draft of the poem in order to "confirm" the reference of "toiles" to the canvas of a painting or a theater backdrop—a maneuver that could only secure this reading through appeal to authorial intention. Indeed, de Man must even follow Pichois by speculatively altering the draft itself, presuming ("sans doute," Pichois tells us) that Baudelaire wanted to write not "Où peint" but rather "Où se peignent." But even on the grounds of this tenuous appeal to authorial intention, de Man's gestural confirmation fails, since Baudelaire in fact *erased* "peint" and replaced it with "vivent"—which would suggest that these "toiles" are *not* sufficiently understood as a surface whereon something is painted, but must be grasped as that upon which something *lives*: "Des êtres disparus." If anything, the replacement of "peint" with "vivent" would suggest a web rather than a canvas. But more importantly, the alteration of the draft and the text of the published poem itself leave the referent *unconfirmed*. De Man confirms his interpretation by refusing to read the text in front of him.

---

163 de Man, "Anthropomorphism and Trope in the Lyric," 258.

This occlusion of the ambiguity of "toiles" plays a crucial role in de Man's deployment of "Obsession" as a recuperative lyric foil for "Correspondances." He can find no counterpart in the former of the disarticulation he locates in the latter:

> If the symmetry between the two texts is to be truly recuperative, it is essential that the disarticulation that threatens the first text should find its counterpart in the latter....There ought to be a place, in "Obsession," where a similar contrast between infinite totalization and endless repetition of the same could be pointed to. No such place exists. At the precise point where one would expect it, at the moment when obsession is stressed in terms of number, "Obsession" resorts to synthesis by losing itself in the vagueness of the indefinite "Où vivent, jaillissant de mon oeil *par milliers*, / Des êtres disparus aux regards familiers."

De Man refers to this synthetic vagueness of the indefinite as "the reassuring indeterminacy of these infinite thousands." Looking for a place where endlessness would be in tension with totalization, de Man finds that "no such place exists."[164]

But the place de Man seeks is looking right at him, like a purloined letter hidden in plain sight. It directly precedes the lines he cites, precisely as *the place* (où) where those indefinite thousands live: *des toiles*. De Man has already reduced the noun to a clear referent, so he cannot see what we have tried to show: that it harbors a *determinate* indeterminacy; that we *cannot* simply exchange it for a metonymic referent (paintings); that it thus gathers the indeterminacy of "thousands" into *one* place which is also *multiple*. Thus the poem does not "resort to synthesis by losing itself in the vagueness of the infinite." On the contrary, it constructs the very specific *site* of a tension between determinacy and indeterminacy, between the one and the many, between synthesis and division, between articulation

---

164 de Man, "Anthropomorphism and Trope in the Lyric," 259-260.

and disarticulation, between reference and sign. It constructs that site as a signifier. We can say that the *necessity* of the poem resides in the multiplicity of its meanings, but such multiplicity is not merely an appeal to reassuring indeterminacy. It is because the poem *does not* say "peint" that it harbors a multiplicity of meanings making a signifier the site of figural disarticulation, rather than an escape from just that. We know *exactly* where "des êtres disparus" live—*toiles*—but we cannot convert that signifier into a single referent, and thus we cannot secure the metaphorical sense of just what *les ténèbres* are said to be. The poem exists, in the necessity of what is there on the page, insofar as it cannot be made into anything else—just where metaphor would perform that kind of transport. We only "perfectly and quickly understand 'Obsession'" if we overlook the powers of disarticulation it harbors. De Man's great essay is indeed a fine lesson in the mutually constitutive relation of blindness and insight.

Now this use of a signifier to gather the indeterminacy of number into the determinate site of a riven metaphor is essential to the tropological tensions of another great lyric in *Les Fleurs du Mal*, "Le Cygne." Here the central symbol—the swan—gathers the poem's mythical anamnesis together with the living historical memory it inscribes (the passing away of "the Paris of old") into an evocation of the figure of the exile, and thus of Hugo, blending the ancient and the modern through a synthesis of the empirical and the literary suffused with longing. The poem rises to the zenith of lyric emotion even as it falls to the nadir of tragedy, drawing the epic and dramatic into its articulation of insatiable desire:

> Aussi devant ce Louvre une image m'opprime:
> Je pense à mon grand cygne, avec ses gestes fous,
> Comme les exilés, ridicule et sublime,
> Et rongé d'un désir sans trêve! et puis à vous,

> Andromaque, des bras d'un grand époux tombée,
> Vil bétail, sous la main du superbe Pyrrhus,
> Après d'un tombeau vide en extase courbée;
> Veuve d'Hector, hélas! et femme d'Hélenus!
>
> —
>
> And so before the Louvre I am oppressed by an image:
> I think of my great swan, with his mad gestures,
> Like the exiles, ridiculous and sublime,
> And gnawed by an insatiable desire! and then of you,
>
> Andromache, from the arms of a mighty husband fallen,
> Lowly chattle, under the sway of superb Pyrrhus,
> Bowed in a trance beside an empty tomb;
> Widow of Hector, alas! and wife of Helenus![165]

Standing before the Louvre in Haussmann's reconstructed Place du Carrousel—at the site of a geographically and historically determinate place and time—the speaker is oppressed by the image of the swan as the movement of his thought folds it into an association with exiles and then together with his recollection of Andromache.

From the oppressive weight of this image, which bears the conversion of the city into allegory and of cherished memories into stones—the poem then spirals out into enumeration, articulating the plurality of those figures to whom the thought of the swan-exile gives rise:

> Je pense à la négresse, amaigrie et phtisique,
> Piétinant dans la boue,
> ...
> À quiconque a perdu ce qui ne se retrouve
> Jamais, jamais! à ceux qui s'abreuvent de pleurs
> ...

---

165 FE, 292-297.

Je pense aux matelots oubliés dans une île,
Aux captifs, aux vaincus!...à bien d'autres encor!

—

I think of the negress, gaunt and consumptive,
trudging in sludge,

...

Of whoever has lost what cannot be found
Never, never! of those who drink their own tears

...

I think of sailors forgotten upon an isle,
Of the captives, of the vanquished!...and of many more!

The enumeration of particulars gives way to the evocation of the innumerable—the "many more" of whom the speaker thinks—just as "Obsession" evokes the indeterminate "thousands" of beings who burst from the speaker's eye even as they live within *les toiles*. And just as in "Obsession," this evocation of indeterminate number occupies the place of a specific sign—"cygne"—which is itself torn between the determinate materiality of the signifier and the problem of its reference. Here that referent would seem quite clear: "le cygne" refers to the swan which the poem describes over three quatrains. However, as soon as the word is articulated, spoken, its sound refers us also *to* its sound and to its inscription, "le signe," such that the referent becomes the signifier itself. What results is a rift within the sign: insofar as it is seen, it is a word, not a swan. Yet insofar as it is heard, we are referred not only to the swan but also to the written sign. The homophonic sound of the word captures its referential sense by returning it to the image of the word itself, which *does* differentiate "cygne" from "signe," but only insofar as it is read as *cygne*, as a material inscription rather than its referent. The allegory of the poem plays out amid this ruin of reference, this return of the image from ideality to materiality, which makes cherished memories more weighty than rocks. As soon as the image of those memories is spoken it is riven between allegory and stone, meaning and mute material, even as it soars toward those limits of figuration where all genres intersect. The sign is "gnawed by an insatiable desire" insofar as it is nothing other than itself, just where we would have it be everything and everyone. The "toiles" of "Obsession" is something like a miniature of the colossal and insistent *thinking* of the sign we find in "Le Cygne" ("I think...I think...I think..."), a more diaphanous version of the latter's weighty allegory: it holds together at least three referents, such that the thousands of vanished beings living within it find the unity of their home disarticulated in its articulation. They too are exiles, displaced from the self-evidence of the sign that would inscribe the image of their belonging...

We are now in a position to register one of the simplest things about "Obsession," which accounts for the complex significance of the concession (*Mais*) with which the final tercet begins. It is *the sound* of "des toiles" which brings back the stars wished away in the previous tercet, "étoiles." The physicality of rhyme, its phonetic taking place, amounts to a renunciation of the absolute: "Comme tu me plairais, ô nuit! sans ces étoiles" / "Mais les ténèbres sont elles-mêmes des toiles." *Plairais* rhymes with *mais*, gratuitously, before we hear the return of the stars, those impediments to pleasure, through the necessity of end rhyme, which demands their sound in the signifier: *des toiles*. And didn't we want them all along, the light of their "langage connu?" *The darkness is itself those stars* that we had wished away, since the extinguished candles of *ténèbres* carve them in the mind's eye even after they are put out, and since, within the poem, their name is written in ink. They live in the sound of the signifier as they burst from the eye that sees the darkness of the sign, pronounces it. Oinos hears *the syllables* of thousands of friends in the tones of the voice of the Shadow, and it is the *characters* of his writing that Baudelaire sees—"jaillaissant de mon oeil"—as he inscribes a canvas already covered in the mind. Those disappeared beings of the sonnet's last line are thoughts become signs, like those

"Milles pensers dormaients, chrysalides funèbres" that are released in "Le Flacon," "Frémissant doucement dans les lourdes ténèbres." It is the conversion of memory, of thinking, into writing—one must hurry slowly—that is the site of mourning and recognition in the final tercet of the poem, as it is in "Le Cygne." And that conversion is *mourned*—it has this feeling—because that which is remembered is not recalled: the determinacy of the signifier *is* the indeterminacy of meaning, such that the referent remains recessed, ambiguous and latent. The writing of the sign makes it what it is, rather than what we could exchange it for. But if there is a sense in which that is always the case, it only becomes significantly manifest under certain conditions. It is indeed true that if the next line said "Où se peignent" then the reticent complex we have been reading would go missing. It is the silence of what the poem does not say that makes it what it is, that allows the *existence* of poetry to tremble within the obduracy of the letter. But this trembling is not a "reassuring indeterminacy." The sign is there, it exists, and it is perfectly determinate: it is the determinate place where indetermination lives. That is why we cannot exchange it for what we wanted to say.

Indeed, the word "toiles" calls to mind the whole problem of exchange, in its historically specific resonance. As Baudelaire writes "Obsession" in 1860, having written "Danse Macabre," "Les Sept Vieillards," "Les Petites Vieilles," and "Le Cygne" within the space of a year, Karl Marx is setting to work on *Das Kapital*. That book will begin with a chapter on the relationship between coat and linen, taking up the question of value through the production of woven textiles. One would not be entirely mistaken in thinking this is what the book is *about*. The value of the coat *seems* to be the value of those materials from which it is woven, or the use to which it can be put. The commodity disguises the *metaphor* of value by dressing it up as the *metonymy* it is not. That metonymy would be the relation of material (canvas, filament, thread) to use value (painting, trapping, decorating). But the secret of commodity exchange lies instead in the conversion of *time* into *value*, which does not inhere in the metonymic relation of materials to the use of the object into which they are fashioned, but rather in what can only be grasped as a metaphor whose substance is social. But if there is a parable of labor recessed in the word "toiles"—in the weaving of a web, the production of the substrate of a painting, or the tailoring of curtains that adorn the chamber of a noble hall—then it does not operate on the level of reference. In order to snap into focus as a referent, "toiles" needs a proximate object or activity: *peint, d'araignée, rideau*. It needs a metonymy in order for the metaphor to travel from tenor to vehicle. Instead, the transit of the metaphor is interrupted by the obstacle of non-identity, by the problem of *what the metaphor is made of*, the indeterminacy of *that which is woven*—canvas, web, or curtain. One of these is *natural*: the spider's web does not accrue value through socially necessary labor time, only through its use to the spider. Two of these are *social*: canvas and curtain are products of human labor, though the value of a painting *on* the canvas will be differently determined than that of the canvas itself, or of a sable drapery. Bound up in the question of the meaning of the word is thus the question of whether or not it refers to a commodity, and of what sort of commodity its referent might become. That is: there is a sense in which the word refers to the problem of the commodity per se and its relationship to meaning. The ambiguity of "toiles" communicates a rift between nature and culture, object and art, concrete and abstract labor through the determinate indeterminacy of reference latent in the poem's final strophe.

But how do we preserve this rift when we interpret? Consider Walter Benjamin's influential readings of Baudelaire, wherein the elaboration of motifs presents a series of figures of the commodity. In "Central Park," Benjamin tells us that "the stars in Baudelaire represent a picture puzzle of the commodity. They are the ever-same in great masses."[166] But insofar

[166] Walter Benjamin, "Central Park," trans. Edmund Jephcott and Howard Eiland in *The Writer of Modern Life: Essays on Charles Baudelaire*, ed. Michael W. Jennings (Cambridge: Harvard University Press, 2006), 137.

as the stars *figure* this picture puzzle, they are inadequate to its puzzling quality. The stars are wished away in "Obsession" for precisely this reason: their light speaks a language we already know; it is not the language of the new. Perhaps, as Benjamin argues, the stars are akin to commodities insofar as they are "the ever the same in great masses." But unlike the commodity form analyzed by Marx, they do not seem to contain sufficient mysteries, and are thus banished in pursuit of pure indetermination. Perhaps the puzzle of the commodity lives where we are not looking for it, and perhaps it is not legible as a *picture puzzle*, but rather in the ruse of a signifier that never locks into representation, in the unfolding of a metaphor whose vehicle captures its tenor in the discrepancies of what it does not say, rather than conveying it toward the coherence of an image. If, like Benjamin, we proceed to read the prostitute as the figural incarnation of the commodity, or if we argue that "the shock experience which the passerby has in the crowd corresponds to the isolated 'experiences' of the worker at his machine,"[167] then we recuperate the instability of modernity through the stability of representation. That is, we *reify* that instability as a stable correspondence, a figure, an image. For Benjamin, Baudelaire's line from "Une Passante"—"A flash...then the night!—Fugitive beauty"—*figures* modernity as the fleetingness of fugitive figuration. On the other hand, the line—"Mais les ténèbres sont-elles mêmes des toiles"—resists the reification of the figure it does not quite convey, despite presenting itself as the very model ("sont elles-même") of metaphor. This model is undermined as it is instantiated. And this gives us occasion to question whether a *figure* of the commodity could really convey the negativity, the social abstraction, of its determinations. Might we do better to limn the contours of reification where it is *not* represented? Perhaps *representations* of the commodity are a poor locus for thinking through the ideological force of reification, since

---

167 Benjamin, "Some Motifs in Baudelaire," trans. Harry Zohn in *The Writer of Modern Life*, 192.

figural sense often requires reification rather than teaching us to undo it. Marx deploys many metaphors, but he also analytically dismantles and theoretically re-elaborates social hieroglyphs in a manner suggesting that the critique of aesthetic ideology—the critique of reified figuration—is an indispensable element not only of literary criticism but also the critique of capital.

Of course, it is Paul de Man himself who points us to the material existence of the signifier while criticizing what he calls "aesthetic ideology": the absorption of figural rhetoric through a synthesis of the imagination producing correspondences between words and things.[168] But we are insisting that we may locate an implicit resistance to aesthetic ideology in "Obsession," an obstacle to the transport of metaphor, rather than reading the poem as the recuperation of "a complementary relationship between grammar, trope, and theme,"[169] as does de Man. What is at issue in "the rhetoric of romanticism" is the power of the imagination to figure its own limits, to overcome those limits through metaphor. In the Romantic tradition Baudelaire extends and delimits, the word "ténèbres" is a major signifier of such figuration. In Gautier's poem, *Ténèbres*, it becomes the sign under which apocalypse is represented. And in Hugo's great sequence, "Au Bord de L'infini," we set out from the sentence "J'avais devant les yeux les ténèbres." The edge of infinity begins with darkness, with shadows, with spiritual doubt, and these *are there* before the speaker's eyes. Imagelessness is presented as image. Translating literally to retain the position of the pronouns:

---

168 See Paul de Man, *Aesthetic Ideology*, ed. Andrzej Warminski (Minneapolis: University of Minnesota Press, 1996).
169 de Man, "Anthropomorphism and Trope in the Lyric," 261.

J'avais devant les yeux les ténèbres. L'abîme
Qui n'a pas de rivage et qui n'a pas de cime
Était là, morne, immense; et rien n'y remuait.
Je me sentais perdu dans l'infini muet.
Au fond, à travers l'ombre, impénétrable voile,
On apercevait Dieu comme un sombre étoile.

—

I had before my eyes the darkness. The abyss
Which had no shore and which had no summit
Was there, bleak, immense; and nothing stirred therein.
I felt myself lost in infinite muteness.
At bottom, through shadow, impenetrable veil,
One descried God like a somber star.[170]

In Hugo's poem, "les ténèbres" flows easily into "l'abîme." In the Romantic imagination, and often in Baudelaire's, the term is potentially exchangeable for a series of signifiers—abîme, gouffre, l'ombre, muet, etc—all of which portend, in one way or another, the spiritual crisis of the retraction of God evoked by Hugo. Yet in "Obsession," we find "les ténèbres" *differentiated* from this chain of equivalences—from "le vide, et le noir, et le nu"—by the qualification of "mais," and it is at precisely this moment of differentiation that the word becomes the tenor of a metaphor transforming it into that *something else* which it itself is. The figuration of the limits of the imagination, the figuration of a concession to these limits, is itself delimited by the failure of the figure to compose an image. Hugo's speaker has "les ténèbres" *before my eyes*, but when "les ténèbres" are figured as "des toiles," the torn sign into which this shadowy darkness is incorporated transforms it into something other than what is there before me. If I register the split referent of "des toiles," then what I have before my eyes is not the projected image of a referent,

---

170 Victor Hugo, *Oeuvres poétiques* II, ed. Pierre Albouy (Paris: Pleiade, 1967), 721. My translation.

but a material signifier that becomes an obstacle to metaphorical unity. Determining "les ténèbres" through its indeterminacy, "toiles" becomes the site of the signifier at which the figuration by the imagination of its own limits is captured and woven into a formal complexity exceeding the parameters of imagination per se. Such complexity requires *analysis* and *exposition* in order to exist: it exists only insofar as we make the dislocation of the sign and the metaphor an object of knowledge. If such analysis does not make that complexity exist, does not separate the existence of the poem from the unity of creative intention and receptive intuition, then the poem falls back into metaphorical transport, into the manifestation of aesthetic ideology that it in fact resists.

The exemplary reading of Les Fleurs du Mal through the ideological relay between creative intention and receptive intuition is that of Jean-Pierre Richard in Poésie et Profondeur.[171] We say "exemplary" because Richard's phenomenological essay, "Profondeur de Baudelaire," is among the finest interpretations of Les Fleurs du Mal we have encountered, as subtle and philosophically rich as it is beautifully written. But how does Richard proceed? He traces relations among images and "sensible schemes" in Baudelaire's oeuvre in order to limn the mysteries of analogy between spirit and reality it explores. The hidden jewel, the glimmering of light through mist, interior shadows held in tension with heliotropism, the lustre of the sea, the transparent yet obdurate substance of a pane of glass (*la vitre*), the expressive flows of blood and fire and tears, the relation between putrefaction and the spiritualization of matter: all of these Richard draws from the poems, persuasively, as elements of "le monde baudelairien"[172] which is also "le drame intérieur de Baudelaire"[173] and "la mystique baudelarienne"[174]—a

---

171 Jean-Pierre Richard, *Poésie et Profondeur* (Paris: Éditions du Seuil, 1955).
172 Richard, *Poésie et Profondeur*, 116.
173 Richard, *Poésie et Profondeur*, 93.
174 Richard, *Poésie et Profondeur*, 114.

shifting terrain of sensations to be lived through the receptive imagination of the reader. Relations among these images, textures of sensation, and logics of elemental mediation are drawn out of the poems and recomposed in the seductive lucidity of Richard's prose, such that "la sorcellerie évocatoire," by which Baudelaire defined poetic writing, becomes Richard's own method. As Richard acknowledges, this evocative sorcery "rests entirely upon a linguistic optimism."[175] "To each of these landscapes," he says of Baudelaire's sensory worlds, "corresponds a rhetoric," and this correspondence "would have been impossible if between language, mind, and reality, there did not exist, *a priori*, certain internal relations, certain analogies of structure." "Verbal architecture," Richard continues, "must rejoin a sensible architecture if one would pass seamlessly from a phrase to a reality and a reality to a phrase."[176] What we have tried to show by elaborating a pivotal line in "Obsession" is that, on the contrary, Baudelaire's poetry arrives at its most complex determinations when it resists the linguistic optimism of seamless analogy, when its figurative levels resist the synthesis of imagination, and when—regardless of authorial intention—the poem disarticulates the evocative sorcery of metaphor just where it insists on it. For Richard, the interior hollow of conscience is "the space of ecstasy and vertigo which constitutes the locus of Baudelarian *spirituality*," but Richard will try to show how this hollow, or cavity (*creux*), is "replenished and humanized" by the "activity of the imagination."[177] This recuperative movement formulates the activity of the imagination in terms of humanist ideology, a direct relay between the compositional activity of the poet and the receptive experience of the reader via seamless correspondences between word and thing. Such humanism will always try to recuperate the sickness of Baudelaire's flowers by watering them

---

175 Richard, *Poésie et Profondeur*, 160.
176 Richard, *Poésie et Profondeur*, 159.
177 Richard, *Poésie et Profondeur*, 95: "Ce creux, on verra comment l'activité de l'imagination parvint en effet chez Baudelaire à le remplir et à l'humaniser."

with good intentions. When we produce an analysis of poetic *determination*, rather than the transparency of correspondences within imagination, we read not in terms of creation, intention, or technique—and not in terms of the relation between "content" and "form" (which may always be subsumed back into the relay between technique and intention)—but at the specific level of poetic existence rather than its expressive cause. The analysis of poetic determination grasps the resonance of poetic signs in their non-identity both to what is said and what is not said, that strange exteriority of signs to reference which makes the poem what it is.

Rather than reading the obstacle to metaphor we encounter in the determination of "les ténèbres" through the lens of *intention* (as an obstacle Baudelaire deliberately constructs), perhaps we might consider "des toiles" as what Deleuze calls an "involuntary sign." Again, the final tercet of the poem seems to be "about" such signs: the registration of gazes that "burst from my eye." The strophe situates us on the brink of madness, where we find "involuntary signs that resist the sovereign organization of language and cannot be mastered in words and phrases, but rout the logos and involve us in another realm."[178] Perhaps the final tercet of "Obsession" attempts a *representation* of madness, or could be read as such: the speaker plunging from his preference for a starless night and his pursuit of absolute vacancy into a disturbing encounter with "those vanished beings" whose familiar gazes inhabit the very absence of determination he had sought, showing its emptiness to be replete with teeming, shadowy traces of undead life. Yet the *way* in which this putative representation transpires renders it irreducible to representation, and renders dubious the scene of representation itself. This is only appropriate, since madness cannot be represented; it is precisely that which evades and cancels powers of representation. The tercet can be grasped as an *instance* of madness, of obsession, only insofar as it is *not* a representation thereof, but

---

178 Deleuze, *Proust and Signs*, 173.

is rather the site of an involuntary sign that skews and disorders the metaphorical rendering of the limit of Romantic imagination, *ténèbres*. It is the resonance of this sign, "des toiles," within and throughout the ideological field it transforms that renders it involuntary: though he is certainly capable of the intentional deployment of ambiguous signs, we do not mean to speculate that Baudelaire set out, in this line, to displace the metaphorical synthesis of a major Romantic signifier. It is the capacity of involuntary signs to circumvent the productive and receptive power of imagination that renders them signs of a possible or inchoate madness, and here the delirium is that of the poem itself, rather than a psychological state represented by its author or imagined by its reader. Just as it cannot be represented, madness is unimaginable.

When Gautier comes to assess the achievement of *Les Fleurs du Mal*, he recognizes that the complex determinations of such a book have to be approached through the mediation of authorial intention and historical context by the *literary* history through which it emerges. "Literature is like the day," Gautier writes: "it has a morning, an afternoon, an evening and a night."[179]

> Il est dans chaque littérature des époques où la langue formée à point se prête à merveille, après le balbutiements de la barbarie, à l'expression limpide et facile des idées génèrales, des grands lieux communs sur Dieu, l'âme, l'humanité, la nature, l'amour, la vie, la more, tout ce qui fait le fond même de la pensée humane. Rien n'est usé alors, ni les sentiments, ni les mots. Toute métaphore semble nouvelle, aucune comparaison n'est fanée encore; les rapprochements les plus directs étonnent par leur hardiesse.[180]

---

[179] Théophile Gautier, "Préface aux *Oeuvres complètes*" (1868) in André Guyaux, ed., *Baudelaire: Un demi-siecle de lectures des Fleurs du mal (1855-1905)* (Paris: Presses du l'Université Paris-Sorbonne, 2007), 476.

[180] Théophile Gautier, "Baudelaire" (1862) in Guyaux, *Baudelaire*, 352.

In every literature there are epochs wherein perfectly formed language lends itself marvelously, after the stammerings of barbarism, to the limpid and easy expression of general ideas, of great commonplaces concerning God, the soul, humanity, nature, love, life, morality, everything that constitutes the foundation of human thought. Nothing is worn out, neither feelings, nor words. Every metaphor seems new, no comparison has yet faded; the most direct connections shock with their boldness.

But Baudelaire does not belong to the facility of such a dawn, to an epoch of classical perfection. Situating Baudelaire as a poet of the evening, of what Baudelaire himself will call "The Sunset of Romanticism," Gautier characterizes his style through a brilliant redefinition of decadence. "In our eyes," he writes, "what one calls decadence is on the contrary complete maturity, the extremity of civilization, the coronation of things," characterized by "an art supple, complex, at once objective and subjective."[181] He returns to this theme six years later, in his Preface to the 1868 *Oeuvres Complètes*:

> Le poète des *Fleurs du mal* aimait ce qu'on appelle improprement le style de décadence, et qui n'est autre chose que l'art arrivé à ce point de maturité extrême que déterminent à leurs soleils obliques les civilisations qui vieillissent: style ingénieux, compliqué, savant, plein de nuances et de recherches, reculant toujours les bornes de la langue, empruntant à tous le vocabulaires techniques, prenant des couleurs à toutes les palettes, des notes à tous les claviers, s'efforçant à rendre la pensée dans ce qu'elle a de plus ineffable, et la forme en ses contours les plus vagues et les plus fuyants, écoutant pour les traduire les confidences subtiles de la névrose, les aveux de la passion vieillissante qui se

---

181 Gautier, "Baudelaire" (1862) in Guyaux, *Baudelaire*, 352.

déprave et les halluncinations bizarre de l'idée fixe fournant à la folie. Ce style de décadence est le dernier mot du Verbe sommé de tout exprimer et poussé à l'extrême outrance.

—

The poet of *Fleurs du Mal* loved what is improperly called the style of decadence, and which is nothing other than art arrived at that point of extreme maturity which determines aging civilizations through the oblique rays of their sun: a style ingenious, complicated, knowing, full of nuances and researches, forever expanding the limits of language, borrowing from all technical vocabularies, taking its colors from all palettes, notes from all keyboards, striving to render the thought within that which is most ineffable, and the form in those most vague and most fleeting contours, listening in order to translate the subtle confidences of the neurotic, the avowals of aged passion that depraves and the bizarre hallucinations of the idée fixe giving rise to madness. This style of decadence is the last word of the Word summoned to express everything and carried to extreme excess.

This must still be the finest description of *Les Fleurs du Mal* we have. When Gautier asks, rhetorically, "Le couchant n'a-t-il pas sa beauté comme le matin?" ("Does the dusk not have its beauty like the morning?"), he asks after the beauty of his own tribute. Gautier sees in the dense intricacy of Baudelaire's style the *determination* of a social world through rays of the setting sun. We translate *déterminent* literally in order to mark the specificity of this claim. It is because literary history has reached a point of extreme maturity that a literary work—by a poet who *loves* what is called decadence, who affirms and is adequate to its complexity—can render all the contradictory determinations, the obsessions, the refinements, the madness, and the passing shadows of the age in which he lives. We see in a line like "Mais les ténèbres sont elles-mêmes des toiles" the simple yet infinitely complex amplitude of that capacity, which traverses the poet as he traverses the city with a gait, so it was said, akin to that of a spider, as he hurries slowly to cover the canvas before setting pen to paper, as he spends years translating Poe "because he is like me." If we have found in "Obsession" the production of a tautology—the tenebrous determination of *sont elles-mêmes des toiles*—we may find also that emotion which resides, for Benveniste, within the interiority of poetic language. It will not be the emotion *of the poet*, but perhaps of the sentiment which moves him, which comes from elsewhere and determines the feeling of what is written, like those feelings "for which there is no name on earth" to which Poe's narrator alludes, nameless feelings born of a plague year. In Baudelaire's poem, "toiles" is the no name of those feelings, the sable web of their covered canvas, wherein live disappeared beings at once familiar and unknown, sounding as they are seen.

It is the existence of the poem we are trying to locate in the resonant obduracy of the signifier, at once determinate, ambiguous, expressive, and mute. It is difficult to locate because the poem is not its form, nor its matter, nor the feeling of its reception. The sign exceeds its materiality even as it sinks back into it. Form is qualitatively abstract, or a formal feeling, even as the synthesis of its unity must return to its composition by discrete marks, which never quite settle into coherence. To disarticulate the unity of matter and meaning, form and feeling, while holding together the *determinacy* of the gap or rift the poem constructs, would be to suspend poetic language in the element of its existence. To sustain that suspension as we elucidate the parameters of its tension: that would enable us to elaborate the work while leaving it as it is.

Envoi

One morning, having walked for a long time along the outskirts of a dim city, you pass aimlessly though an open gate, up several stairs attended by mythic creatures crouched in stone upon the lower pillars of the banisters, between the columns of a simple portico, and step through the unlocked door of a seventeenth century hall. Something draws you into this conspicuously abandoned place, the mystery of its vacancy. Across a checkered floor, up the grand marble staircase to the first level and down a hallway hung with portraits of some defunct noble line, a lofty door of brass, set ajar, opens onto a large chamber, ensconced in gloom, with black curtains shutting out the light of day and the view of the empty streets outside. But seven iron lamps illuminate the scene, their flames left burning by the last occupants. Their tall, slender lines of light rise up the walls and cast their lustre upon a large ebony table in the center of the room, the black surface of which reflects their glow. Goblets of wine have been left half full, casting shadows upon the inky depth.

Seven chairs circle the table, pushed back from its edge, with one left fallen sideways upon the floor near a linen shroud that lies heaped between the chair and the folds of the sable draperies obscuring the windows. In one corner of the room, a narrow wooden desk is pulled close to a divan heaped with crimson pillows. A long-extinguished pipe sits beside an inkwell from which a tall white quill extends in an arc. Is it the feather of a swan? A book sits open, extending just off the edge of the desk, while another sits atop a folder of papers on a green folio with a silver corner.

To the right of the divan, an armoire stands against the wall, vaguely sinister in its regal bearing. The doors turn reluctantly on their hinges as you open them to an acrid odor, a scent of sorrow and forgetfulness. It is empty but for three objects set on a dusty shelf: an old flask of emerald green blown glass with a crusty stopper, a camphor coffer with a rusty lock, and an iron key. You pick up the flask, and already a pestilential scent wafts into the air as you nevertheless work the stopper out of the top and hear a faint rustle amid the draperies across the room, as if an insensible quiver had passed through the somber atmosphere. Chilled, you set the stopper back in the flask and place it deep into the corner of the armoire, where it is lost in darkness. Then you take the key and try the lock of the coffer, which creaks as if in complaint at the disturbance. But it turns, and you open the lid to find within only a small rectangular piece of paper, with a single phrase written out by hand in an elegant script: *Mais les ténèbres sont elles-mêmes des toiles.*

You place the paper back within the coffer and return it to its shelf, closing the armoire and drifting back over to the corner where you sit down at the desk, sinking into the divan and picking up the book to inspect its contents. On the recto leaf to which it has been left open, page 179, you see the same phrase printed at the head of a sonnet's final tercet, which reads in full:

Mais les ténèbres sont elles-mêmes des toiles
Où vivent, jaillissant de mon oeil par milliers,
Des êtres disparus aux regards familiers.

The lines remind you of something. As if looking for it, you begin to flip through the volume, at first glancing here and there, eyes flickering over thousands of characters, then reading slowly, immersed in poem after poem. As the hours pass by and the lamps light your way, you tap out the bowl of the pipe on the desk and fill it with the tobacco you have in the left pocket of your jacket, lighting it with the matches in your right pocket, and then you return to the strange and singular volume, its languid and caustic tone mingling with the residual scent from the flask and with the smoke now gathering into a whorl as you read.

It must be evening by now; you don't have a watch, and the clock on the wall is stopped at 7:08—but perhaps that could be right, or will be soon. It is as though the words begin to drift into the air, or as if the dormancy of the room begins to invest the pages with its haunting emptiness. At length you set the book aside for reference, your mind suffused with its uncommon mood, and then you draw a blank sheet from the folder of paper on the green folio, pushing the latter back to make room on the desk. Taking the white quill from its well, whose ink is still fresh, you reflect for a moment, dwelling within the passage of time through the space you have entered, and then you begin to write.

Montréal, April 10 – May 18, 2020

INDEX OF POEMS

All Entire (*Tout entière*), 137

Balcony, The (*Le Balcon*), 130, 154
Beauty (*La Beauté*), 113–115
Benediction (*Bénédiction*), 131–132

Carrion, A (*Une Charogne*), 127–128, 173–174
Cat, The (*Le Chat*), 117
Confession (*Confession*), 98
Correspondences (*Correspondances*), 118

Damned Women (*Femmes damnées*), 110
Danse Macabre (*Danse macabre*), 94–102, 127
Destruction (*La Destruction*), 71–73

Eccentric's Dream, An (*Le Rêve d'un curieux*), 179
Enemy, The (*L'Ennemi*), 38, 68
Evening Harmony (*Harmonie du soir*), 67, 122–123
Evening Twilight (*Le Crépuscule du soir*), 110
Exotic Perfume (*Parfum exotique*), 129–130

Fantastic Engraving, A (*Une gravure fantastique*), 89–94, 110
Flask, The (*Le Flacon*), 117

Gambling (*Le Jeu*), 110

Hair (*La Chevelure*), 124–125
Heauton Timoroumenos (*L'Héutontimoroumenos*), 68–69, 133
Hymn to Beauty (*Hymne à la Beauté*), 50, 112–113

I have not forgotten (Je n'ai pas oublié), 36–37
Ideal (*L'Idéal*), 67
Invitation to the Voyage (*L'Invitation au voyage*), 117
Irremediable, The (*L'Irrémédiable*), 70–76

Jewels, The (*Les Bijoux*), 82, 122

Lethe (*Le Léthé*), 82, 144
Little Old Ladies, The (*Les Petites Vieilles*), 143–158

Martyr, A (*Une martyre*), 174
Mask, The (*Le Masque*), 48

Obsession (*Obsession*), 62, 108, 167, 170–200

Phantom, A (*Un fantôme*), 174
Pipe, The (*La Pipe*), 117
Previous Life, The (*La Vie antérieure*), 81, 118

Sepulcher (*Sépultre*), 176
Seven Old Men, The (*Les Sept Vieillards*), 25–54
Song of Autumn (*Chant d'automne*), 103
Spleen—Pluviose (*Spleen*—Pluviose), 87–88

Swan, The (*Le Cygne*), 107, 185–188
Sympathetic Horror (*Horreur sympathique*), 111

Taste for Nothingness, The (*Le Goût de néant*), 85–86
To a Creole Lady (*À une dame créole*), 80–81
To the Reader (*Au Lecteur*), 137
Two Good Sisters, The (*Les Deux Bonnes Soeurs*), 157

Voyage, The (*Le Voyage*), 48, 107, 121
Voyage to Cythera, A (*Un voyage à Cythère*), 131–143

INDEX

abyss, 159–171
aesthetic experience, 123–134
aesthetic ideology, 192–196
allegory, 24, 28, 69–72, 84, 92, 101, 106–107, 116, 142–143, 186–188
apocalypse, 88–102

beauty, 49–50, 88, 93, 98, 107, 112–116, 122–130, 135–136, 142–144
Benjamin, Walter, 190–192
Benveniste, Émile, 119–120, 159–166

cats, 96
colonial synesthesia, 128–134
commodity, 191–192
Culler, Jonathan, 69

De Man, Paul, 168, 181–185, 192
death, 13–25, 52–54, 88–102, 103, 138–139, 153–154, 167
decadence, 197–200
Delacroix, Eugène, 52–54
Deleuze, Gilles, 177
Deren, Maya, 176

ekphrasis, 88–102
enchantment/disenchantment, 134–158
existence of the poem, 38–39, 168–171

Flaubert, Gustave, 148–150
free indirect discourse, 144–152

Gautier, Théophile, 108–109, 167, 197–199
glimmer, 111–118
God's fearsome claw, 156–157

honeybee, 151–152, 157
Hugo, Victor, 143, 192–193

imagination, 43–46, 51, 69, 89–94, 101, 112, 129, 192–197
irony, 68–88, 97–98, 101–107, 120, 122, 125–128, 134

Kane, Sarah, 162
Kant, Immanuel, 55–69
Kyger, Joanne, 177

Laplantine, Chloé, 159, 163

Macherey, Pierre, 168–171
Mallarmé, Stéphane, 159
Marx, Karl, 189, 192
materiality of the Signifier, 159–200
Miller, G.A., 30–31
Mortimer, John Hamilton 89–94

nothing, 21–23, 55–71, 76, 79, 81, 88–96, 101–102, 139
number, 17–39, 187, 203

Poe, Edgar Allan 13–25, 178–181
poetic determination, 11–12, 23, 29–34, 69, 76, 81, 83–84, 88, 107, 132, 142–144, 157, 164, 168, 171–173, 180, 184, 189, 194, 196, 200
poetry, 98, 104, 132–134, 158, 165

race, 79–84
reading, 9–12, 201–203
reason, 51, 55, 59–69, 92, 102–103, 112–113
Richard, Jean-Pierre, 118, 194–196
riddles, 152–155

Satan, 69–76
saturation/suspension (grammar), 35–40
shadow, 9, 13–25, 49, 58, 81, 108–111, 116–117, 166, 174–175, 178–181, 201
spirit, 143–158
spleen/ideal, 65–69, 103
subject/object (grammar), 171–173

toiles, 172–200
truth/actuality, 146–148

void, 62–102

Whitehead, Alfred North, 162–163
Williams, William Carlos, 104–107
writing, 13–25, 76–79, 203

Nathan Brown is Professor of English at Concordia University, Montréal, where he is founding director of the Centre for Expanded Poetics. He is the translator of Baudelaire's *The Flowers of Evil* (Verso, 2024) and the author of *Rationalist Empiricism: A Theory of Speculative Critique* (Fordham, 2021) and *The Limits of Fabrication: Materials Science, Materialist Poetics* (Fordham, 2017).

IDIOM: INVENTING WRITING THEORY
Jacques Lezra and Paul North, series editors

Werner Hamacher, *Minima Philologica*. Translated by Catharine Diehl and Jason Groves

Michal Ben-Naftali, *Chronicle of Separation: On Deconstruction's Disillusioned Love*. Translated by Mirjam Hadar. Foreword by Avital Ronell

Daniel Hoffman-Schwartz, Barbara Natalie Nagel, and Lauren Shizuko Stone, eds., *Flirtations: Rhetoric and Aesthetics This Side of Seduction*

Jean-Luc Nancy, *Intoxication*. Translated by Philip Armstrong

Márton Dornbach, *Receptive Spirit: German Idealism and the Dynamics of Cultural Transmission*

Sean Alexander Gurd, *Dissonance: Auditory Aesthetics in Ancient Greece*

Anthony Curtis Adler, *Celebricities: Media Culture and the Phenomenology of Gadget Commodity Life*

Nathan Brown, *The Limits of Fabrication: Materials Science, Materialist Poetics*

Jay Bernstein, Adi Ophir, and Ann Laura Stoler, eds., *Political Concepts: A Critical Lexicon*

Willy Thayer, *Technologies of Critique*. Translated by John Kraniauskas

Julie Beth Napolin, *The Fact of Resonance: Modernist Acoustics and Narrative Form*

Ann Laura Stoler, Stathis Gourgouris, and Jacques Lezra, eds., *Thinking with Balibar: A Lexicon of Conceptual Practice*

Nathan Brown, *Rationalist Empiricism: A Theory of Speculative Critique*

Gerhard Richter, *Thinking with Adorno: The Uncoercive Gaze*

Kevin McLaughlin, *The Philology of Life: Walter Benjamin's Critical Program*

Alenka Zupančič, *Let Them Rot: Antigone's Parallax*

Adi M. Ophir, *In the Beginning Was the State: Divine Violence in the Hebrew Bible*

Ronald Mendoza-de Jesús, *Catastrophic Historicism: Reading Julia de Burgos Dangerously*

Jacques Lezra, *Defective Institutions: A Protocol for the Republic*

Massimiliano Tomba, *Revolution and Restoration: The Politics of Anachronism*

Chunjie Zhang, *The Quest for Liberation: Philosophy and the Making of World Culture in China and the West*

Nathan Brown, *Baudelaire's Shadow: On Poetic Determination*

www.ingramcontent.com/pod-product-compliance
Lightning Source LLC
Chambersburg PA
CBHW020409080526
44584CB00014B/1246